ARGUING
with
GOD

'The Lord said to Job:
"Shall a faultfinder contend with the Almighty?
He who argues with God, let him answer it." '

Job 40: 1–2

ARGUING
with
GOD

CHRISTIAN CLASSICS SERIES

The problem of evil

by
Hugh Silvester

Inter-Varsity Press

INTER-VARSITY PRESS
38 De Montfort Street, Leicester LE1 7GP, England

First published 1971
First published in Christian Classics, 1996

British Library Cataloguing in Publication Data
A catalogue record for this book is available from the British Library.

ISBN 0-85111-236

Printed and bound in Great Britain by Cox & Wyman Ltd, Reading,
Berkshire.

*Inter-Varsity Press is the book-publishing division of the Universities and
Colleges Christian Fellowship (formerly the Inter-Varsity Fellowship), a
student movement linking Christian Unions in universities and colleges
throughout the United Kingdom and the Republic of Ireland, and a member
movement of the International Fellowship of Evangelical Students. For
information about local and national activities write to UCCF, 38 De Montfort
Street, Leicester LE1 7GP.*

CONTENTS

INTRODUCTION

This is really written for Christians. It has been said many times that there is no 'problem' about evil and pain for someone who does not believe in a loving God. For the unbeliever, who perhaps in the last analysis defines evil as 'what I do not like', there is no problem of evil but only a world which contains many unpleasant features. He may try to eliminate them, or some of them, but he can have no sense of 'injustice' or 'unfairness' in the way in which these evil things are distributed. He is wasting his breath to complain (unless of course the complaining is publicly done to bring about some reform), because in his view there is no-one to complain to.

But the Christian *does* have someone to complain to. And even if he may not be as honest as Job and complain directly to God in prayer, he will sometimes diffidently, sometimes rebelliously, complain to his friends that it doesn't make sense that a loving God should have allowed so much trouble in the world. Or again, in discussion the thinking Christian may be confronted with what one philosopher has described as 'perhaps the most powerful of all sceptical arguments', which may leave him bewildered and distressed. It may be that, in summarizing some of the arguments that have already taken place, this book will help him to hold his own in debate. Being a Christian, however, is not a philosophical game and this book also contains some pointers as to how the Christian should cope with suffering and deal (or ask God to deal) with evil in his own life and world-view.

But this book is also written for those unbelievers who, for varying reasons, are considering becoming Christians. And part of the cost of that decision will be to believe in a loving God while living in a world in which there are many unpleasant features. If you become a Christian then you will have on your plate a first-class philosophical problem. You can, of course, at this point commit intellectual suicide. Faced with the sceptics, you can wave your hands and say 'It's a great mystery' and quite happily live the Christian life in company with a great unsung army of believers who do not worry about the problem, either because they do not have the intellect to grapple with it or more usually because they are much too busy living and loving to bother with second-order questions. I do not wish to suggest that this large group of believers is somehow 'second-class'. Rather I would say they are fortunate if indeed they are never worried by such awkward questions. But many of us *are* worried, both before and after becoming Christians, and it is for those that I offer these arguments and pointers.

Two more things by way of introduction. First, I shall frequently refer to the Bible, its statements and its charac-ters, assuming that what is written there is true. It is my own conviction that the Bible is God's way of revealing Himself to us. I use my reason and philosophy to think round and through what God has said. If I cannot make sense of what is said, then I take it that my reason is lacking and not that the record is faulty. It is perhaps significant that there is very little 'argument' in the Bible. Its stand-point is vastly different from that of Plato who thought of man's highest function as the exercise of reason. There is no space here to consider my reasons for my conviction except perhaps the negative one that philosophy has shown itself over and over again to be full of arguments but lacking in conclusions. No sooner does one person erect a water-tight system than another comes with his logical marlin-spike to puncture it. Disturbed as we are by awkward questions, very few of us desire merely stimulating intellectual games; we want to know the truth, or as much of the truth as we are able to bear. Without the concept of revelation we are merely 'raising the dust only to complain that we cannot see'.

Second, I am aware that some will be reading this with some particular evil or tragedy in mind, the death of a loved one, for instance. Others may be emotionally shocked or disturbed by medical work, or by a national disaster, or by the baffling problem of 'Why me?' 'Why did it have to happen to . . . ?' If what follows seems cold and analytical, I can only say that it is vital that we try to think things through on this level first. Our minds must control our emotions, not vice versa. And, for the Christian, the mind must be informed by what God has said, not by wishful thinking or by sentimental optimism. Certainly we shall want to apply the arguments to actual situations. But this I shall have to leave largely to you, for suffering is too personal, too individual, for me to try to generalize or to dole out wholesale advice. And in any case, I am concentrating on the problem of *evil* rather than the problem of *suffering*.

Third, it is commonly assumed by sceptics, and all too readily conceded by Christians, that it is the sceptic who asks all the awkward questions. Of course it is impossible to disturb the complete agnostic, for in answer to every question he returns a bland 'I don't know'. But it is my contention that there are a great many awkward questions to which we all want to know the answer and there *is* a Christian answer to a good many of them. This is not to say that Christianity arose as a system which answers awkward questions, nor that to be intellectually satisfied is a good

9

reason for becoming a Christian. But if God *has* revealed Himself in Jesus and the Bible, then we shall expect that revelation to answer many of the queries we feel compelled to raise.

At the end of each chapter I have put one or more of these awkward questions. The Christian can ask his sceptical friend, the enquirer can ask himself, first, does he really want to know the answer and second, has he got an answer which is satisfying?

1 THE DEFINITION OF GOOD

Subjective and objective

Only too frequently men argue with each other. They argue
because they disagree. Sometimes they disagree about facts,
sometimes about the interpretation of facts and sometimes
about the relative values of objects, facts or states of affairs.
Even more they disagree about people.

There has grown out of these arguments a rough distinction between objective truth and subjective truth. When
an argument is about something which can be settled by
empirical evidence, then the truth is said to be 'objective'.
For instance if I say it is 104 miles from London to Bath,
my friend disagrees and says it is 100 miles. First we must
clarify our terms ('What do you mean by London? Aldgate
Pump? Buckingham Palace?'). Then it is merely a matter of
measuring the map, or driving the distance with a reliable
milometer. Once this has been done we shall agree: the
truth of the matter is 'objective', that is to say it lies outside
and independent of either me or my friend.

It is possible to agree about facts and yet to disagree
about different interpretations of those facts. I understand
that astronomers agree that the nebulae are rapidly moving
away from each other. But they do not agree as to what may
be inferred from this. Some say that long ago there was a
'big bang' and that we are now looking at the tail-end of
the explosion. Others say that matter is being continuously

created which keeps the universe in a 'steady state'. Equally intelligent men are arguing about interpretation: their theories are 'subjective' – that is they imply a bias on the part of the thinker which makes him (the subject) choose a certain theory as being true. Fresh evidence is being sought for the confirmation of these theories but, until such empirical facts emerge, the two rival theories are 'subjective'.

But disagreements about value are more intractable. Sometimes there is an objectivity about value. For instance if a man cannot get more than £300 for his second-hand car it is no good at all his saying that it is 'worth at least £450'. 'Worth' to whom? Not to himself, because being the owner he is not in a position to buy it. Nor to anyone else apparently, since he cannot get an offer of more than £300. The market value is an objective figure.

But grand arguments, for which there seems to be no referee, rage when people argue on topics such as music. If a man A says that Beethoven is better than Bach and his friend B disagrees, there seems to be no possibility of objective agreement. If B argues that the counterpoint in Bach is more satisfying, A merely retorts that it is the repetitious counterpoint that he finds so particularly distasteful. Questions of fact cannot be brought in to settle arguments of value: the opinions are (almost) entirely subjective. This man values Rowland Hilder: the other, his voice dripping with contempt for bourgeois art, values Paul Klee. This man likes playing golf on Sundays: the other would prefer to go to church.

So in all areas of life where there is disagreement which cannot be resolved by 'look and see' methods, we find men making value judgments which would seem to be subjective. In ancient philosophy it was assumed that there must be some kind of standard or prototype value which men were looking for and which they were arguing about. This is certainly not acceptable to present-day linguistic philosophers, who say that all words and language which contain hidden or plain value judgments are subjective. There may be descriptive or factual elements in such language but basically the language is expressing a preference and the speaker is inviting the hearer to share his attitude.

What is 'good'?

The word 'good' is the supreme example, they say, of such 'inviting' or emotive language. Containing no factual elements, it is 100 per cent value judgment and thus completely subjective. It is true, of course, that if I say 'This is a good watch', it implies not only that I like this watch, but that it will keep time within acceptable limits and we can reasonably assume that anyone wishing to own a watch also wishes it to keep time. In certain contexts the word 'good' can have factual inferences. But when the word 'good' is applied to a person, it carries no agreed factual content whatsoever. If a concentration camp commandant had said of an S.S. trooper 'He is a good man', most of us presumably would have flatly disagreed. The word 'good' in that context is entirely subjective, because it is entirely rooted in the speaker's own values.

If 'good' then is subjective it would seem that the definition of good is 'what I prefer or value' (*e.g.* 'That is a good play'/'It's been a good day'/'Good dog!'/'Rasputin was a good man'). Conversely 'evil' means 'what I disapprove' (*e.g.* 'That was an evil lie'/'He is an evil boy'/'It was an evil day when I got married'). The position however is not so simple as this. 'Good shot!' while watching football is merely ejaculating – expressing my approval and pleasure at what I have just seen. But this is not to say that that is always what 'good' means. If a schoolmaster says 'That was a good punishment' it does not mean that he enjoyed beating the boy: he may have loathed doing it. But he is

13

expressing an over-all approval of the system of corporal punishment. Many people will agree with him, and he lives and acts within this context that he is not alone in his approval. If he were the *only* educationist who felt like this about punishment he could find himself hard put to it to say boldly 'That was good punishment'; he would probably say 'That was *what I call* a good punishment'. He would go out of his way to draw his hearers' attention to the fact that he was using 'good' in a purely subjective sense.

There grows up in our minds, then, a pretty shrewd idea of what most people approve, and so the word 'good' acquires a certain objective content. No-one pretends that this is a universal standard. Sometimes, instead of 'most people', it must become 'most Europeans' or 'most educated people' or 'most cultured people' or 'most Christians' who approve this, that or the other. Do any of these 'objective' standards provide us with a guide for value judgments? Philosophically they do not. People talk a lot in these days of 'declining standards', but what is the original standard which they applaud and what is the super-standard by which conflicting standards are judged? And yet in spite of the philosophers we have a feeling about people and right conduct that we do not have about buildings and their shapes. We feel that there must be an objective standard for man. Let us try and put this special feeling into words.

The good man

One line of argument that has been put forward is that the special feeling about moral judgments arises from the fact that we are men and thus not only talking about other people but include ourselves. If we make a moral statement about, say, stealing, we are prescribing a pattern of behaviour for ourselves. As this is a momentous undertaking it gives us a special sense of solemnity.

This may be part of it. It is true that when I meet either in the flesh or in writing a man whom I immediately and instinctively call 'good', I have a longing to be like him. But we can go on and ask *why* I long to be like him. And it seems that there is about that life a certain Socratic 'fitness': we feel that we are looking not just at a man but at Man as he ought to be. I do not merely approve of him, I am *drawn* to him. To know him is to love him and to want to be loved by him. In other words the objective/subjective distinction becomes blurred as I become involved in another person. My word 'good' refers to something because there he is, in front of me – in his 'goodness'. But my knowledge of him is intensely personal. 'Subjective'? Yes, but none the worse for that!

Personal knowledge of a 'good' man is a great deal more than approving of a man I happen to meet in the train. It is one of the great experiences that life has to offer. That obituaries only occasionally capture the experience should not blind us to the reality. Personal knowledge of a good man brings its own certainty: it does not require a standard by which to judge the goodness. You do not argue with a third party about a good man. If the third party disagrees, you just say 'I'm sorry, but you don't know him'. That's all. It never occurs to you (as it might in an argument about Beethoven) that you might be mistaken or have faulty judgment. You *know*. And you know that he's good.

God is good

Jesus made this remarkable statement: 'Why do you call me good? No one is good but God alone.'[1] Now if God exists then it is reasonable to suppose that He is the standard by which all value must be judged; that He contains within

[1] Mark 10:18.

Himself the objectivity which men have been hankering after. It is outside the scope of this book to discuss whether or not He exists – our title presupposes that we can argue about Him or against Him or with Him. Assuming Him then to be, He must be the source of all value by which people or states of affairs are to be judged. If God 'approves' then the thing is 'good' and if He 'disapproves' then it is 'evil'.

Christians claim that knowledge of God is personal. Jesus certainly taught it. He claimed that He knew God as Father while His antagonists, the Jewish religious leaders, did not. Does this make religious truth 'subjective'? Yes, in so far as all personal knowledge is subjective. But for the subject himself God is very much 'there' and objective in a degree which makes other 'objects' insubstantial.

But God is not just another person. He is God and the ontological source of all things. He is not merely the source of value pronouncing one thing 'better' than another. He is the very *raison d'être* of that thing: 'In him all things hold together.'[2] And immediately we fall into a dilemma. Things exist because God pleases, and what pleases God is 'good'. Therefore everything that is must be good. All the unwelcome facts of life such as disease, cruelty, crippled children, ugly words, insecurity, infidelity, corruption, perversion, manipulation, fraud and so on; all these must be part of the 'good' will of God otherwise they would simply cease to exist. If God withdraws their *d'être* they would have no *raison* to be there as objects.

Immediately common sense reacts. If this is theology then we want no part in it. 'Most decent men' simply do not approve that list of horrors. Am I to call them 'good' because some despot in the sky pronounces them to be so? I will never submit to such a monster though he has absolute power! Already we are arguing with God if not shouting at

[2] Colossians 1:17.

Him. He is Creator: He is responsible for everything that exists. Some of His works are splendid: life can be very good. But what business has He to allow so many evil things in the world? And then, literally adding insult to injury, He tells us we must call them 'good' simply because He happens to approve of them: He demands that we violate our own natural judgment (which presumably He has given us) and pronounce things 'good' when we feel in our bones that it is not merely something that we disapprove of but something that is *evil*. Take any example of brutal torture, such as repeated drowning and bringing back to life. Everything in us cries out that this is 'monstrous', 'unnatural', 'inhuman': to say I disapprove is a masterpiece of meiosis. Men who do such things are not fit to live. I can feel no mercy for such felons. And yet these things happen, but only because God allows them to exist. This makes us feel, not like arguing with God, but shaking our fist at Him.

Fatalism

Some religions, notably Islam, appear to try to defend God in situations like this by a folding of the hands accompanied by 'It's God's will'. You see a man in the road with a broken leg: it is God's will. You cannot do anything about it. If you are ill it is no use to get medical help. If it is God's will for you to recover, you will, for He can heal without the aid of (Western) medicine. On the other hand, if it is time for you to die, you can do nothing to avert death. It is God's will (*kismet*).

The effect of this doctrine is twofold. First, it has an eroding effect on man's compassion. Life is hard, we know that. But it is daily eased by a hundred and one kindnesses that come from men who oppose evil and fight it, whether it is a physical evil such as hunger, or a spiritual evil such as injustice. If 'God's will' is conceived in this depressing and omnibus fashion, it weighs down on every merciful man. What can he do? How dare he do it? He might even find himself, like Paul, 'fighting against God'. But the second and far more serious effect is the image we are given of God: inscrutable, doling out good and bad fortune with little or no reference to the characters of the recipients, having motive and purpose completely unknown and unknowable. How can you love such a God? The answer: you must not love Him, you must worship Him, honour Him, obey Him, fear Him and hope that He won't notice you.

It is not only Muslims who think like this about God. It is possible for a Christian to take words from say Isaiah 55:8, 9, and expound them in the same spirit: '. . . my thoughts are not your thoughts, . . . my ways are higher than your ways . . .'. Many have suffered at different times from so-called 'Calvinists' who go far beyond Calvin in describing to us a God almost indistinguishable from Allah, the 'all-merciful'. Jesus talked about His Father's will as a way of discovering the truth of His own teaching; as something He accepted for His own personal destiny; but not as a *carte blanche* for every evil that might exist. It is no doubt proper and Christian to say in the right context 'It is God's will' and to fold the hands: but to say it piously when you hear that six million Jews have been murdered is blasphemy.

When Jesus was arrested He said 'This is your moment — the hour when darkness reigns'.[3] There are times in life when evil itself seems to take over and be the ruler over the affairs of men. That Jesus felt like this when He saw Himself and His truth being overwhelmed in an outburst of vindictiveness is plain. Paul similarly testified to 'this dark world . . . the superhuman forces of evil in the heavens'.[4] This is not just a first-century superstitious fear of demons

[3] Luke 22:53, NEB.
[4] Ephesians 6:12 NEB; *cf.* also John 9:4.

and spirits: it is this unavoidable conviction that there is real, naked evil abroad. Churchill described it in his speech in 1940 when he spoke of the possibility of '. . . a new dark age . . .'.

Nowhere in the Bible do we find such evil designated 'good'. Evil is opposed to God and to His followers. In Isaiah 5 we find a series of woes pronounced on evil-doers and one of them is:

> 'Woe to those who call evil good
>   and good evil,
> who put darkness for light
>   and light for darkness,
> who put bitter for sweet
>   and sweet for bitter!'

It helps no-one to say of an evil 'It is God's will' if by that we mean 'what you call evil, God calls good'. We may not be able to understand God completely but this is different from saying that we cannot understand Him at all. And if evil is 'good' simply because it exists, then indeed God is incomprehensible. He is not worth defending: such a theodicy, a defence of God's ways, is senseless because it cannot be tested by any normal criterion.

The Creator is responsible

Part of the difficulty lies in the fact that we fail to notice that 'will' is a complex notion and is frequently used in complex situations. Take for instance the catch-phrase 'I disagree passionately with what you have said, but I will defend with my last breath your right to say it'. This is a complex situation. If you asked the speaker whether he 'approved' of his opponent speaking in this particular way he would emphatically deny it. He would do anything to stop such pernicious views being published. Anything? No: he would not like to see a police state (not even one run by himself and therefore just honest, truthful, *etc.*) where people were unable to express what they were really thinking. The speaker thus approves of free speech, but he does not approve of the use that his antagonist is making of it.

Is it good that carving knives should exist? Most people round about 1 *p.m.* on Sunday would say 'yes'. But this does not mean that they approve of Mr X doing away with his wife at the same time with the same implement.

I am going to call these two kinds (or levels) of approval First and Second Order Approval. We give 'Carving-knives' our First Order Approval but we withhold our Second Order Approval from 'Murder-by-carving-knife'. Approval of free speech as an institution is a First Order Approval; we will such an institution to exist. But that does not mean we must approve every scatter-brained sentiment that is bandied about.

At first sight it would seem possible to argue that God wills things to exist, that He gives them His First Order Approval, but this does not mean that He approves everything within creation. Whether or not this is a valid argument depends on how far it is possible for a creature to be independent of or free from the Creator. It might be one thing to say that a man withholds his Second Order Approval from a particular action because the objective existence of that action does not depend on his approval. But it might be a very different thing to extrapolate such a situation into God who presumably need not tolerate anything that He disapproves of. Is man free? Is this really the best world order that could be arranged? These are the kind of questions that begin to arise as we start arguing with God.

Summary

Let us summarize so far:

1 'Good' and 'evil' are subjective words in normal conversation.

2 When I use 'good' of a man, this is a personal experience which removes the subjective/objective distinction.

3 If God is a person, His 'goodness' will be grasped only by personal experience.

4 If God exists, *His* approval is the standard by which we judge.

5 This does not mean that when God says 'good' it can mean the opposite of what men mean.

6 'Good' and 'evil' situations are often complex and so is the notion of 'will' in relation to them.

7 First Order Approval of a large context does not necessarily mean Second Order Approval of everything that appears within that context.

QUESTIONS FOR FURTHER THOUGHT OR DISCUSSION

What is your ultimate basis for 'value' judgments?

Is there an objective basis for moral judgments? If not, why do we often argue as if there were?

2 TWO TYPES OF EVIL

Assuming God's existence, and accepting for the moment that He has made some creatures 'in his own image', the worst kind of evil that you could find would be the deliberate rebellion of such a creature against its Creator. This creation and rebellion are described in Genesis 1-3: how should we understand these stories?

Evil as rebellion

Some interpreters say that the story is 'myth'; that is to say, it holds moral truth but is not historically true. The truth the Fall story contains is that everyone, as a matter of fact, has rebelled against God and His lawful commands and has failed to keep the law of love. So the Fall did not happen once but it happens to everybody every day.

Now I would not deny that this particular truth is contained in the story but I think there is nothing to be gained by abandoning the historical event. First, it is worth noting that there is no scientific evidence which disproves the idea of a Fall in the year X BC. There is every indication that the world-wide spread of *homo sapiens* started from a single source. Physiologically, the human race is one: blood groups, pulse rate, anatomy, inter-fertility of different ethnic groups, *etc*. The chances of two or three groups emerging simultaneously at different points in the world and then being physically compatible is indeed remote. Differences of skin colour, shape of face, *etc.*, are superficial. Anthropologically to posit the existence of a single ancestral pair (possibly New Stone Age Man) is not only reasonable but likely. For most people geology has of course upset Ussher's dating of the creation of the world, but dates are not part of the Bible narrative. In an interesting book[1] V. Pearce has drawn together and compared the biblical narrative with modern anthropology and those interested could pursue his bibliography.

The difficulties of a historic Fall are not scientific but logical and theological. The main logical difficulty is this: how could man in a state of perfection and goodness and in communion with God commit an act of rebellion? This logical difficulty, which seems to create evil *ex nihilo*, will be dealt with in greater detail in chapter 5. It is perhaps sufficient to note at this point that knowledge of the good and the right is not sufficient of itself to make us choose it. In some inexplicable way we all seem to have a bias away from the good.

Let us summarize the teaching from Genesis 1-3:

1 God made everything (chapter 1).

2 Everything was made 'good' (1:31, *etc.*).

3 Man was made 'in the image of God' (1:27).

4 Man was told to subdue the earth and was given 'dominion' over all living things (1:28).

5 Man was given a choice (2:16, 17).

6 A tempter (the serpent) tried to persuade the woman to sin (3:1-5).

7 Man and woman disobeyed (3:6).

8 Pain in childbearing, bitter work and expulsion from the favoured place was the result (3:8-19).

9 'Death' is the result of the sin (2:17).

[1] *Who was Adam?* (Paternoster Press, 1969).

Point 1 is to be expected, but it is remarkable that there is no hint of dualism: *everything* is from God. He is not a master craftsman grappling with obtuse 'stuff'. Point 2 reminds us that it all had God's approval as it left His hand. In some sense it had a perfection that it does not necessarily have now. Points 3-5 emphasize that it was man's special position which gave his act its special evil quality. Made like God, he aspired to be '*as God*'. It was the most outrageous act that can be imagined. In the twentieth century we think of the worst sins as those that harm (innocent) man. Evil, properly understood, is first and foremost an act against God.

Some have argued that we should draw a distinction between the 'image' of God and His 'likeness', that the 'image' is that we are capable of having fellowship with God and that the 'likeness' is the final perfecting of the character to be actually like God. This implies that even before the Fall man was somehow 'lacking' and forms the basis of an evolutionary theology. It is difficult, however, to sustain this difference on etymological grounds and the summary verse (1:27) merely uses 'image' repeatedly.

There would seem to be at least three things implied about man being made in the image of God – *i.e.* characteristics not shared by the animals:

1 The ability to *understand* (power of reflection or theoretical reasoning).

2 The ability to *choose* (an agent, not an instrument).

3 The ability to *love* (a self-conscious preferring of another before oneself).

The tree was fenced with a mere word. A plain choice was set before the pair. They could put God first – or themselves.

Man is not improving

Here, then, is the biblical account of the origin of evil. The history of the people of Israel that follows underlines one gigantic lesson. They were specially chosen by God to be His vehicle of blessing to the rest of mankind; they were given His word or law. But repeatedly and persistently they renounced their vocation and rebelled against Him. Psalm 78 is a gloomy summary of their spiritual pilgrimage. Far from getting better, far from having more and more advanced ideas of God, far from moving from a primitive ignorance to an advanced sophistication, they set themselves deliberately and systematically against God and His purposes. A few quotations from the Psalm make this abundantly clear:

> They did not keep God's covenant.
> They refused to walk according to His law.
> They forgot what He had done.
> Yet they sinned still more against Him.
> How often they rebelled against Him.
> They turned away and acted treacherously like their fathers.

The story of the Old Testament is not an account of man's evolutionary improvement but of his failure. The prophets, who were repeatedly sent to recall the Jews to their lofty destiny, were ill-treated. Finally the exile into Assyria and Babylon took place in fulfilment of all the warnings. One of Ezekiel's main themes in Babylon is that 'you are a rebellious house'.

The message of the Bible, therefore, is about evil. And the main and primary evil that is spoken of is rebellion against God: the creature setting himself up against the Creator. Man had every chance. He had God's law. He knew God's purpose, and he rejected it. This is the first evil.

It is interesting to note that many rulers who were outstandingly evil, from Herod Agrippa to Adolf Hitler, have tried to claim that they are 'as God'. But it is not just rulers who have been at fault. All evil behaviour by man to man implicitly contains the same claim.

Evil in society

If, then, the first great type of evil is rebellion against God, the second is hatred of our fellow-men. Jesus summarized the law into two great commandments:

Love God.
Love your neighbour.

When we leave the first kind of evil we fall straight into the second. Perhaps now we are on more familiar ground: for everyone knows how brutal and evil man can be to man.

There is the individual misery caused by quarrelling. Broken marriages are the result of people being unable to put the other person first. Some quarrels are carried on in a more dignified way than others, but the intention to hurt and injure is there, deep and cancerous. Theft, adultery, slander, dishonesty, backbiting – everyone has his own list with his own personal faults figuring high in the order. It is a fact of experience that we are most skilful at diagnosing and detecting those faults in other people which are our own worst failings. Preachers scold their congregations for spiritual pride; slothful teachers chide their pupils for unpunctuality; greedy parents are quick to notice when their children take too much sugar.

No-one needs a catalogue of the horrors of war – or the bestiality of soldiers. People are shocked and surprised when they read that American or British soldiers have behaved like Russian or Japanese soldiers. What is really surprising is their surprise. Thousands of years of war have not improved man's ambitions. The Assyrians were perhaps the most organized and scientific in their brutality, but some of the Nazis in World War II run them a close second. The myth is that some people, British, American, 'freedom-loving people', are not like that. I read on the wrapper of an English book published in 1943 that 'people like the Germans do not beat people like us', and the author was committed to proving the proposition that English people are somehow decent, clean-living, chivalrous and I suppose Christian, while their enemies got up late, never washed, hated the countryside, and dared to lay their hands on women-folk! Perhaps not many people believe that proposition nowadays. At least they would not admit they believe it. But the danger in the myth is still very apparent.

Evil in myself

In myself I fail to see the evil that is so blatantly obvious in other people. If circumstances permit, for instance in war or a negro riot, it is most convenient to pin the vices on to a whole ethnic group. But in less turbulent times we still have our scapegoats. It may be another church down the road if we are Christians, it may be the staff or the administration if we are students. It may be just the people next door if we are bad neighbours, or That Man in the office without whom life would be (almost) perfect. It is never us, it is never me. If I wish to say something unpleasant to another person I may start by saying, 'I think it is my duty to tell you . . .'. But my duty rarely extends to self-criticism. 'Home truths' never seem to come home.

The vast collective misery of existence which accompanies war, slavery, social exploitation, despotic systems, persecution, insurrection, power-struggles, comes from the evil of the individual man. Comparatively innocent people suffer: but are they completely innocent? Homeless families are a tragedy: but is it less a tragedy to watch a child of four years trying to push a sister out of her rightful place of love in the home. 'Telling tales', a universal childish vice, implies first that the offender has in fact done something wrong and second that the 'tale-bearer' is already odious with a hypocritical self-righteousness. What hope is there for an adult world when its children are so twisted? Human nature is best observed in the nursery. We do not grow out of selfishness, pride, spite, cruelty; we merely learn to keep them within acceptable limits. A good citizen is one who keeps the law: he does not have a perfect heart.

God detests 'social' evil

Without much reflection we would call all these things evil, but to be consistent we should try to relate them to the approval/disapproval of God. In ancient pagan religions it was almost unthought of that your god would interfere with your social or moral life. The god's place was in his temple and he was satisfied with the proper ceremonial. True, misfortune could come on you in everyday life if you scorned him in some way, but by offering a ritual it was possible to keep 'god' in his place.

The Israelites were beginning to think the same about the Lord God, with their grand choirs, splendid music and multitudinous offerings. Amos the prophet bluntly said they were mistaken. God cannot be bought off; ceremonial does not satisfy Him. He wants justice in the courts and fair dealing in the market-places. Not only Israel is castigated but the surrounding nations who may not have the Jewish Law, but are presupposed to know a moral standard.

In the early oracles of the book of Amos the following crimes are condemned: physical brutality; enslaving a whole tribe; breaking of agreements; unsatiated revenge; ripping up of pregnant women; rejection of an accepted standard; sexual promiscuity. God cares about these things, He does not 'approve' and repeatedly He cries 'I will not revoke the punishment'. This close connection between morality and religion which all now take for granted was forged by the word of God on the anvil of the Hebrew prophets. All sins which hurt man are against God because we are desecrating His image in ourselves.

It is not wrong to be an iconoclast, a breaker-down of images, when the image is that of the idolater. But when the image of God in man is real and we crumble it away, then it is not only an assault on the sculpture but an insult to the sculptor.

Moral evil and natural evil

What I have just described is usually called Moral Evil. For ease of reference I would like to designate its two forms:

EVIL A The rebellion of man against God
EVIL B The ill-treatment of man by man

Moral evil (comprising both A and B) is evil which comes from man himself. God is 'responsible' for this evil as Creator, but if we are arguing with God we might find that we were also accusing ourselves. But there is another group of miseries and unhappiness which apparently arise outside man – what is often called Natural Evil. I would like to divide Natural Evil into two main groups and for the sake of clarity I will designate them C and D:

EVIL C Those evils which come from the disease-death environment, catastrophic events such as earthquakes, inhospitable regions of the earth (e.g. those with a low rainfall).

EVIL D Animal pain and suffering which possibly includes the case of idiot children. The whole natural order of 'the survival of the fittest'.

Now we call C and D 'evil' because like A and B they cause human misery and unhappiness. But this is to abandon the only plain definition that we have of 'evil', that is, evil is what God disapproves. It is not so easy to establish that 'natural' situations are disapproved by God. Let us first of all notice that the word 'evil' already has a different flavour. Supposing there were two brothers and on the same day one was struck by lightning and the other was expelled from school for stealing. Here are two disasters which will doubtless bring misery to their parents, two evil events. But can you say that the thunderbolt was 'evil' in the same sense that the corruption of this other boy's moral character was evil? Indeed the thunderbolt should be compared to the headmaster's action, and the latter was not evil at all, but just. Similarly, it is very difficult to maintain that an owl which kills a mouse is evil unless of course you are writing a book in which all the heroes are mice, in which case you are deliberately projecting your own human feelings into a mouse situation. It may suit your literary purpose but it tells us nothing about the thoughts of an owl!

Another way of talking about this different 'flavour' of the word 'evil' in moral or natural contexts is to say that it is possible to argue that C and D are not necessarily disapproved by God. After all, death is only a gateway to immortality and you do not have to go and live in an inhospitable region. Animals may enjoy being chased and hunted by their natural predators. I am not saying that these are good arguments, only that they are possible arguments. What is quite impossible is to argue that evils A and B are approved by God. There is an 'evilness' in their very essence which makes it absurd to talk of these evils as 'disguised good'.

God is responsible

The difficulty with Natural Evil is that God, if He exists, is directly responsible. The avoidance of this charge has been classically met by suggesting that evils C and D are the result of man's Fall. Man as the crown and master of creation became corrupt and 'dragged down' the whole edifice with him. This is nowhere stated in the Bible, though there are some passages which might be construed in this way. For example when Paul says 'sin came into the world through one man and death through sin'[2] it would seem to imply such a doctrine. But fossil evidence demonstrates beyond reasonable doubt that animals were dying and dead long before man appeared anywhere. Paul himself adds 'and so death spread to all *men*' (my italics) and a reference to Genesis 3 will remind us that although immediate 'death' was promised as a result of sin, Adam did not in fact physically 'die' in that day. It can well be argued that the death Paul speaks of is the 'real' death of which the grave in this world is only a picture, albeit a very solemn one. But it need not be asserted that mortality as part of this animal-world environment arose only because of the Fall. After all, to an innocent, death from this world would be most welcome. (A detail which supports this view is that the tree of life, also pictured in Eden, was *not* man's possession even before the Fall.)

As for geological and meteorological conditions these are implicit in the very nature of the planet from the beginning of time. The Creator is responsible for these in a way that no-one else is. What are we to think when we read a headline '15,000 people homeless'? Does God really approve of earthquakes? Is it His will that this vast suffering should exist? Are these people more evil than the rest that they should have to bear such a disaster? It is shallow and heart-

[2] Romans 5:12.

less to say that God can teach the people things they would not otherwise learn through such misfortune. Perhaps they would rather not learn them! Besides it is one thing to say that God can bring 'good' out of 'evil', but can we call the 'evil' good? These kinds of argument can quickly drive Christians into defending a God which they do not really believe in. It is the God-of-the-Inquisition who does horrible things to people so that they might be saved. This God is not the Father of our Lord Jesus Christ. If Jesus was upset when 5,000 people were hungry, and at that only temporarily hungry, are we to say that His Father does not care when 15,000 are struck a blow from which many of them may never recover?

In arguing on God's behalf we can find ourselves making un-Christian statements; but if we resist this temptation we find ourselves once more arguing with God as to why He should permit these terrible states of affairs.

Moral evil is a 'bigger' problem

Before I finish this chapter I want to make a point which I think is important. C. S. Lewis estimated that four-fifths of human suffering comes from human beings being wicked to one another. Of course it is only a guess but I think the estimate is on the low side: I would put it at nineteen-twentieths. I suggest these pointers in support:

1 In everyday life the things that cause anguish are people disliking and hating you. Possessions do not confer happiness: nor does the lack of possessions prohibit happiness.

2 Global problems for the most part are caused by wars and selfishness. The planet is able to support us all in moderate comfort; but vested interests, private and public, distribute resources inequitably.

3 Totalitarian regimes based on fear exist because

human nature *is* something to be feared. It is the rulers who first fear and so are determined to rule by fear.

If I am right, 95 per cent of the world's evil can be classified as moral. I am not forgetting those who suffer from the disease-death environment. Pain is painful and no-one enjoys it, but it does not cut and wound like the unfaithfulness of someone you love. We all live under daily threat of sudden death: by bacteria, cancer, blood-clots, lightning, earthquakes, heart failures. But nothing compares to the dread of living in a police state with arbitrary powers of arrest. Until we got used to the idea, we lived in fear of the Bomb, but man never gets used to the appalling indignity and insecurity of living under a tyrant. It is not that with moral evil you can fight it, and with natural evil you accept it; because man continually fights his environment in the research laboratory with sophisticated equipment and on the mountainside with his hoe. It is that moral evil is *really* evil and not just unpleasant.

Without noticing it we have stumbled upon an unwelcome truth. The 'problem of evil' is two-edged. For the aspect of evil which is most repulsive is that for which man himself is responsible. I condemn all these things A and B and yet I still take part in them. If I condemn the secret police then I find myself using their methods in the classroom. I chide my children for being unjust to each other and I myself am partial and selfish. I tell God He has no business to have made the world as it is and look at my handiwork! The first 'problem of evil' is not theoretical and about God: it is practical and about myself.

QUESTIONS FOR FURTHER THOUGHT OR DISCUSSION

What do you do when *you* fail to live up to the standards of behaviour which you yourself have accepted as 'right'?

How do you account for the special 'flavour' of moral evil if there is no God?

3 THE PROBLEM STATED

Anyone who has seen the film *Dr Zhivago* can speak of the gripping way in which it holds up a mirror to life. The bitter and cruel winter in the Ural mountains; the class war with the brutality of the dragoons matched by the ruthlessness of the revolution; Victor's unbridled lust; Zhivago's pathetic unfaithfulness, as he abandons Tanya for Lara. These are the 'facts' of life: in public, in private, in the mass as well as in individuals we see the evil lot of man. Now caught in some historical movement, now constricted by a crippling environment, now driven by some internal demon, man is in an evil state. Is this what God wants? Are we to approve just because it exists?

One of the sceptics, Sextus Empiricus, writing in the second century AD, said:

> 'Those who affirm positively that God exists cannot avoid falling into an impiety. For if they say that God controls everything, they make Him the author of evil things: if on the other hand they say that He controls some things only . . . they are compelled to make God either grudging or impotent, and to do that is quite obviously an impiety'.

A modern philosopher, Alisdair MacIntyre, wrote in 1959:

'If we assert that God is omnipotent we assert that everything that happens happens by His will. And if we assert that He is unqualifiably good we assert that nothing happens by His will except what is good. And these two statements taken together entail that nothing happens except what is good. But the fact that evils occur palpably falsifies this . . .'.

These arguments are similar: both are clear and both seem conclusive. Everyone who has witnessed the death of a child puts the matter more briefly: 'Why does God allow this?' This has been the cry of mothers for centuries. But the depth of the problem appears as soon as we start defending God.

Let us consider each of the four types of evil, A, B, C and D, which I designated in the last chapter.

A The rebellion of man against God

This, the greatest evil of all, is surely the one that God could most easily have avoided. God made man and therefore gave him a nature. Why did He give him such a nature that was able to sin and disobey? When a man makes a machine he builds into it the characteristics that he wants. If he does his maths right the machine will fulfil its maker's purpose. Is God, then, less than man or did He really intend man to take the wrong path? Again, a man might be excused through ignorance: there might be some unsuspected factor at work which eventually ruins his plan. God cannot plead ignorance. For He knows all things, and even if man is going to choose, God knows what man will choose. If then God knew what would happen, why did He create man at all? Why not just leave it or think of something else?

Even allowing that man should take the wrong path how

can he be restored? How can he be saved? Some Christian theologians have answered that by God's irresistible grace a man can be put straight and restored to the image that was his birthright. Why then does not everyone receive this irresistible grace? Why should Simon Peter be rescued and Judas Iscariot be reprobate? If God knew that certain of His creatures were destined to an eternal sentence in hell, we may ask why He created them at all. Is it correct to think of God in some diabolical laboratory dividing people into two groups, rescuing some and rejecting others?

We may notice the use of the adjective 'diabolical' for none other seems to fit. We are not only arguing with God, we are calling Him names. We are saying that His work is the work of the devil and this is very close to the sin against the Holy Spirit of which Jesus spoke when they said He cast out devils by the prince of devils. But in argument terms what we have done is this: we have worked out the conclusions of God being all-powerful and in so doing we have a doctrine of God contradictory to the Christian doctrine. Something has gone wrong. 'Yes,' says the atheist, 'and what has gone wrong is your premise that God exists. There is no God to be thought of as divine or diabolical. The whole thing is a hangover from tribal taboos.'

B The evil of man's inhumanity to man

Quite apart from the fact that we may reap the grim reward of our own wrong-doing, what about the suffering of innocent people? Look at the Jews in World War II. They were no worse than any other section of European society. Why should they have to suffer so wretchedly simply because they bore a certain name? Surely God could have restrained the wickedness of the Nazis? There were plots against Hitler's life by upright German men. Could God not have seen to the success of their plans?

In criminology in the past two or three decades there has been increasing insistence that punishment should be seen as a means of reform rather than an instrument of retribution. It has been argued that a vast amount of crime is the direct result of a poor environment. Poor housing, divorced parents, inflated advertising, careless owners and other things have provided the context where the average person must inevitably succumb to his situation. The argument can be extended in kind to an agrarian situation where the crops fail and a man is 'forced' to steal from his neighbour in order to survive. God did not make man in a vacuum: He provided an environment. Why was the environment He chose such a harsh one?

If, in defending God, I say that man himself is responsible for our twentieth-century crime-incubator, a deeper attack emerges. Whose fault is it that our urban sprawls are what they are? It may be blamed on certain of our ancestors' attitudes during the Industrial Revolution; but why did they decide as they did? Were their decisions not also dependent on *their* environment? Press this argument far enough and it will be seen that God, if indeed He is Creator, willed all things from the first environment He made. You cannot defend Him, as you could a man, by the Rule of Double Effect. This principle applies in a situation where to achieve a good moral result the agent unavoidably and inadvertently perpetrates some bad results. For example an act of surgery may result in a man being crippled for life. The stroke of the knife is 'good' and praiseworthy although we do not approve of the subsequent disability. But as J. Hick has pointed out,[1] the validity of the rule depends on the limited power of the agent. If the surgeon had the

[1] *Evil and the God of Love* (Macmillan, 1966).

power to perform the operation and defeat the disease without unpleasant side-effects, then he would have a duty to use this power. God *has* such power – at least that is what theology leads us to believe – so could He not have avoided the unpleasant side-effects when He created?

Even if we accept that man is primarily responsible for his moral evil, while God is responsible in a secondary and underlying sense, we run into more difficulties. It is a theme of Scripture that God is a Judge: that He decides who is righteous and who is wicked: that He 'saves' or 'delivers' the righteous and punishes the 'wicked'. This theme is found in both Testaments despite some who claim that they can read the Gospels without finding such a theme on Christ's lips.

Now how and when is this judgment carried out? Sometimes it seems that God visits a man or a nation 'in the midst of the years' and deals out judgment through suffering there and then. The defeat and deportation of the Jews in the eighth and sixth centuries BC were unequivocally interpreted by the Hebrew prophets in this way. So in this particular case war (an unmitigated evil brought on man by himself) was used by God as a punishment. Some have tried to extend this to a general principle: that all evil and misfortune are in some way a punishment for sin (*i.e.* moral evil originating in man).

Now if this is so, then quite clearly God's use of evil is a very inexact practice:

First, it is a matter of observation that evil men frequently prosper in this life, while their just opponents suffer greatly.

Secondly, if suffering is a punishment for sin then frequently the punishment is out of all proportion to the offence (*e.g.* a trivial error of judgment in a motor-car can result in the loss of both hands, while systematic oppression by an employer runs unchecked).

Thirdly, people who are relatively innocent, say the children in Hiroshima in 1945, are sometimes subjected to the most appalling suffering.

The psalmist, taking the part of the innocent sufferer, often calls God his 'judge' in the sense of 'saviour' or 'deliverer' and cries out for help. But the observed events indicate that God does not do anything. Why doesn't He? Has He no power or no compassion?

C The evil of the disease-death environment

Man's position on the planet has always been precarious. This is obvious even today with the bushmen in the Kalahari desert or the trappers within the Arctic circle. But it is also remarkable to notice that even a slight upset of the delicate balance of 'secure' civilized living quickly brings hardship and other unwelcome reminders that we live in a harsh world. In a sudden flood or hurricane, all that is cosy in a man's home disappears. The furnishings are wrecked, the car is a write-off, the man may even find himself clinging to the roof in danger of his life.

Another man, secure on the top of the hill in a lush climate, may suddenly lose his child. One day the toddler is prattling happily, the next day he is struck down by a virus which resists diagnosis and the day after he is dead. Life hangs on a slender thread. Death brings personal anguish and suffering to which belief in God seems to bring no comfort.

I would recommend anyone who, like myself, has not experienced an overwhelming sorrow in their own lives to read *A Grief Observed* by C. S. Lewis.[2] The book describes his feelings on the death of his wife and it reveals that personal anguish which is only too easily hidden and not

[2] Faber and Faber, 1964.

understood by those who have 'never had it so good'. He describes his sorrow:

> 'Grief is like a long valley, a winding valley where any bend may reveal a totally new landscape . . . not every bend does. Sometimes the surprise is the opposite one; you are presented with exactly the same sort of country you thought you had left behind miles ago. That is when you wonder whether the valley isn't a circular trench.'

He mentions the disease:

> 'Cancer and cancer and cancer. My mother, my father, my wife. I wonder who is next in the queue.'

He wonders what God's purposes are:

> 'How do they know she is "at rest"? "Because she is in God's Hands". But if so, she was in God's Hands all the time, and I have seen what they did to her here. . . . If God's goodness is inconsistent with hurting us, then either God is not good or there is no God: for in the only life we know He hurts us beyond our worst fears and beyond all we can imagine.'

He faces the crucial question:

> 'What reason have we, except our own desperate wishes, to believe that God is, by any standard we can conceive, "good"? Doesn't all the *prima facie* evidence suggest exactly the opposite? What have we to set against it?'

If these words had been written by an atheist we would have every sympathy: but they were written by a deeply committed Christian. This gives them an extra edge. Indeed it is because a man is a believer that he finds suffering and pain to be a problem. He does not have open to him the retreat of a stoic who faces an impenetrable fate. He claims to have discovered the source of life only to find himself enmeshed in a wretched existence.

D Animal pain: the struggle for existence

A short time ago I was fishing for perch on the Victoria Nile. These fish grow sometimes to 150 lb or more and are caught by trailing a model fish about 6 in long behind a motor launch. Within twenty minutes I had felt about three or four 'bites'. Suddenly I realized what it must be like to be a real fish about 6 in long in the river. Every hour I would have perhaps ten narrow escapes, any one of which could have been fatal. Eventually I caught a fish of about 50 lb. I could hardly lift it on the spring balance and it was about 4 ft long. A monster; a murderer! How many fish had it eaten to attain such a size? Is this another manifestation of the benevolent, powerful creator God whom Christians say is love?

The point hardly needs elaborating that vast numbers of animals and insects maintain their own lives only at the expense of others. Nature is 'red in tooth and claw', as Tennyson said:

> 'For nature is one with rapine: a harm no preacher can heal.
> The May fly is torn by the swallow, the sparrow speared by the shrike,
> And the whole little wood where I sit is a world of plunder and prey.'

When I see a chameleon eating house-flies it pleases me because I detest flies in the house. But when I see a hornbill dragging weaver-bird fledglings out of their nest, it revolts me because I like weaver-birds. How far I approve or disapprove of these slaughterings depends on my ability to identify myself with the victims. And of course I am frequently inconsistent: if I really disapprove the struggle-for-existence in nature, I should be a vegetarian.

And yet in spite of my inconsistencies I feel uneasy. The Royal Society for the Prevention of Cruelty to Animals was founded on a legitimate sentiment: that animals do suffer and can be ill-treated. If I am struck and cry out because I am hurt, then something very like it occurs when a dog yelps on being beaten. If a rabbit screams when it is caught by a fox it is not unreasonable to suppose that something unpleasant is happening to the rabbit. Is 'nature' the best that God can do?

One would have thought that something better could be arranged. Could not all the animals be vegetarian except those scavengers and carrion animals that merely clear up the mess when the others have died of old age? Why should God have instituted a system where life can only be supported at the expense of life? Surely some other form of living could have been devised? The problem of animal struggle becomes sharper when we try to assert that God has made 'the best of all possible worlds'. This phrase does not come from the Bible but from Leibnitz. He argues that God, being the only necessary Being, can produce only one state of affairs and that is the best – an *a priori* argument which hardly appeals to someone who, on looking at 'nature', reckons he can suggest some obvious improvements. Nor is it a matter of detail. The whole principle is 'survival of the fittest' and this in itself seems to be immoral. It means 'might is right' and that to exist is good: gangsters reckon to live in the same way.

Then why should we believe in God?

Having set out some of the arguments and facts which count against the existence of a good Creator-God it might be wondered how belief in Him has arisen at all. How on earth have men inferred from this mass of unpleasant evidence that a good God rules over all? Or, if the question of origin is too remote for investigation, now that the belief has arisen why does it persist? Two catastrophic world wars it is true have destroyed a great deal of conventional belief, but true conviction seems stronger than ever, especially amongst those who have suffered most.

The answer is that men have not inferred this belief. Where 'natural religion' has arisen by inference the picture is of a complex pantheon most of whose members are evilly disposed towards man. Animism and other 'primitive' religions are based on fear of menacing spirits who have infinite capacity to do their worshippers harm. Judaism and Christianity are not 'inferred' religions: their claim is to be 'revealed' religions. They tell us something we could never have guessed unless we were told. Continuing belief in a good God is not supported by intellectual reasoning but by religious experience. Christians believe that the evil in the world does count as an argument against the existence of God as described in the New Testament, but their faith does not rest on observation but on revelation, particularly that given through Jesus of Nazareth.

Should God resign?

After the Aberfan slag-heap disaster in Britain, in which so many young children died, the Chairman of the Coal Board, Lord Robens, offered to resign on the time-honoured principle that the man at the top is 'responsible'. Shortly afterwards a *Punch* editorial was published headed 'Should God resign?' After all, He is at the top and He is responsible. What some unbelievers ask is not 'Should God resign?' but 'Should Christians resign from talking about Him, when the disasters of the world make Aberfan look like a playground?'

Arguing with God

Men are driven to discuss the problem of evil by different circumstances. There are those who see in the problem a final reason for not believing in God at all, and their discussion is aimed only at establishing their own atheism. ('God's only excuse is that He doesn't exist.') There are those, perhaps more sensitive than most, who grieve over the vast suffering of the world, and doubt if it can ever be reconciled with the Christian view of God as loving. The third group are those who would take up cudgels on God's behalf and justify His ways to the world. The fourth and last group, easily the most important, are those who have suffered greatly in their own experience which has driven them to think and say all kinds of things about God.

Perhaps the most famous of the last group is Job whose story is told in the Bible. 'And the Lord said to Job: "Shall a faultfinder contend with the Almighty? He who argues with God, let him answer it" ' (40:2). Everyone who wishes to 'discuss' the problem of evil, even those in the suffering category, will find themselves 'arguing with God'. Even the defenders of the faith who wish to justify God, to produce a theodicy, will find themselves in the doubtful position of saying what God must or must not do, can or cannot do. And this is dangerous.

It is *so* dangerous that it has led some Christians to say that any theodicy is impious; that the infinite God does not require justifying to finite man; and that finite man could not understand the final argument, even if it were presented to him. There is some truth in this; but men *are* puzzled by evil, and suffering is a *fact* and they want to talk about it. And it won't help them to be told 'You mustn't'. Further, we have all been given brains and you cannot find a verse in Scripture to say you must not use them. You must not use any ability in *pride*, but that is different. Austin Farrer, commenting on the fact that C. S. Lewis wrote *A Grief Observed* after his *Problem of Pain* said, 'He who has stood fire may fairly reflect on mortal combat; not, however, while he is dodging bullets. Some people have no use for reflection; but that's another matter.'

If at any time we seem to talk as though everything were plain and open before us, we lie. Job admitted, 'I have uttered what I did not understand', when faced with God Himself (42:3). But it is interesting to note that God did not condemn him for this. God said that Job had spoken of Him 'what is right' and this is repeated (42:7, 8). Theodicy may be undertaken, but with fear: fear of misrepresenting God and fear of God Himself.

QUESTIONS FOR FURTHER THOUGHT AND DISCUSSION

If God exists we have the problem of evil. But if He does not exist how do you account for the fact that it still seems like a problem?

Since the case against the existence of God is so strong why do you think belief in Him has persisted, especially when you consider that believers are found at every intellectual level?

4 SOME UNSATISFACTORY SOLUTIONS

It has been pointed out that the problem of evil can be restated as follows:

Christians assert that three statements are true:

1 God is wholly good.
2 God is all-powerful.
3 Evil exists.

It is not possible to hold all these together without contradiction. If the problem is to be solved then one or more of these statements must either be denied or qualified. As far as possible I shall try to group some of the solutions that have been offered under one of these three statements.

Before I do so, I would like to criticize one extra 'solution', and that is the one which says, 'Yes, they do contradict one another but that is what I should expect if I start to try and understand God.' To say this is to fail to see the difference between paradox and nonsense. A paradox is something that *seems* to be nonsense but in fact contains a truth – like 'the first shall be last and the last first'. But nonsense is nonsense whether you are talking about the weather or about God. Here is H. L. Ellison on the subject:[1]

'The Christian will quite cheerfully discuss the mystery of the Trinity . . . But when you take him by the back

[1] *From Tragedy to Triumph* (Paternoster Press, 1958), p. 61.

of the neck and rub his nose on some of the facts of life
he is promptly up in arms, and appeals to the inscrutable wisdom of God.'

Once the Christian admits that there is a real and complete
contradiction in his thinking he can give up his claim to
talk sense and may logically make any statement he
chooses, however outrageous.

Solutions which deny statement 1

1. 'God is wholly good.' Surely no Christian would deny the
truth of that statement! We noticed, however, in chapter 1
that we can start using the word 'good' about God in such
a way that it is soon taking on a meaning that is far away
from the normal usage. If I say that good=existent, then
war is 'good', because war exists. But this is not what most
people mean by 'good'. So we are saying, 'God is not good
in the ordinary sense, but in the sense that He exists': we
are in effect denying the proposition 'God is wholly good'.

2. Or take this statement: 'God loves me like a father'.
Supposing a human father were given the choice as to
whether or not his small son contracted polio. How would
he decide? To give the answer is superfluous. Yet, presumably God does have this kind of choice in front of Him: and
in some cases does decide that it is 'good' for a child to have
polio. To go on talking about God as a loving father is to
use words in a quite foreign sense. For no father would act
as God seems to act by allowing people to contract polio.
And yet Christians claim that God is their 'Father', though
it is interesting to note that nowhere in the New Testament
is the believer guaranteed freedom from ills.

3. Then there is a suggested solution that the evils of this
life are punishments for sin. This is readily acceptable in
traditional African thought. A man is struck by lightning.

If he was a bad man everyone says that his evil deeds have at last caught up with him: but if he was a good and well-respected man, then he must have perpetrated some secret evil-doing or unwittingly have offended some spirit. You can find this kind of thinking reflected in the arguments of Bildad, one of Job's 'comforters'. Having described all the evils that come by terrors, war, brimstone, and exile he says 'such are the dwellings of the ungodly, such is the place of him who knows not God'.[2]

Although the Western world may be 'civilized', superstition of this kind has a deep hold. Have you noticed that every time you say 'The car is running really well now', within a week you are replacing the brake-linings or fitting a new exhaust? Few people will say 'I have never had a serious car smash' without adding 'Touch wood' or more devoutly 'Thank God'. We are reluctant to make such unvarnished, but indubitably true, statements. Somehow we feel that all we say 'is being taken down and will be used in evidence'.

This attempt to explain the presence of evils falls down in the first place because ills as a matter of observable fact are simply not apportioned fairly to evil-doers; and in the second place by Christ's explicit repudiation of it. 'Who sinned, this man or his parents, that he was born blind?'[3] Jesus answered 'Neither.'

4. Another oblique way of saying that God is not good is by saying that He is 'above' or 'beyond' good and evil, just as He is 'beyond' male and female. To put this another way, God created both good and evil like opponents in a football match, so that men can decide which side to be on. But clearly this takes away the whole flavour of 'good'. In one sense it does not matter whether I am a man or a woman: but I am convinced it matters very much whether I am

[2] Job 18:21. [3] John 9:2, 3.

'good' or 'evil', and part of my conviction rests in a belief that God is irrevocably committed to the side which is 'good'.

Solutions which deny statement 2

'God is all-powerful.' But is it possible that there are some elements within creation which are not subject to His control?

1. In the Gnostic thought of the second century AD creation was conceived as a process or emanation from God in a series of 'aeons'. Each member of the series, as it grew further 'away' from God the source of all perfection, grew 'less perfect' than its neighbour. Thus the final emanation, or demiurge as it was called, was not only imperfect but evil and opposed to God Himself. It was this demiurge that was responsible for creating the present corrupt world order full of evil. That is why it crucified Jesus, reckoned to be a 'true son' or first emanation from the Godhead. Thus God cannot control the demiurge who is responsible for all evil.

The real difficulty at the heart of this explanation is the equation of imperfection with evil. God contains in Himself His own cause and is thus 'perfect' in the sense that none of His creatures is. But to suggest that this somehow makes a remote creature of His to be evil is absurd, for evil means to be disapproved by God. Just because my artefact is not me, it does not justify my disapproving it.

2. If the Gnostics were monistic in their thought, that is they tried to derive evil from God Himself via the idea of imperfection, then Plato's solution was frankly dualistic. Dualism is a metaphysical theory which asserts that the ultimate reality is Two (or more) and not One. Plato thought of God as a master-craftsman wrestling with intractable, hard-to-manage 'stuff' out of which He created all things. In creation God was confronted with conditions

which opposed Him. Quite apart from the fact that Christian orthodoxy rules out the idea of 'matter' as eternally co-existent with God, dualism is most unsatisfactory as final philosophical theory. If God and Matter are the two ultimate realities, what is the relation between them? How did they themselves come to exist or come to be in contact? If neither is stronger than the other there can be no final synthesis. If one is stronger than the other, the conflict should have been already settled if both are eternal. The highest category of purpose makes no sense at all and we are left with these two monolithic giants eternally locked in meaningless combat. Dualism raises more questions than it answers.

The attraction of dualism is that it does seem to solve the problem of evil neatly. Some modern theodicies whilst appearing to be monistic turn out to be disguised dualism. Karl Barth talks of the principle which opposes God as *das Nichtige*, 'the nothingness'. His language is obscure and He revels in contradictions, but this 'nothingness' came into being when God willed to create a good universe. 'Nothingness' was considered and rejected – but because God rejected it, it is not merely 'nothing': it 'has its own being, malignant and perverse'. God brought it into being because He chose this universe. But this immediately raises the question of God's limited power. Could He not have willed this creation without bringing into existence the 'nothingness' which had to be defeated at such tremendous cost on the cross of Christ? If He *had* to choose both, then this is almost dualism, *das Nichtige* just waiting to be brought into existence to fight against God's purpose![4]

3. Another modern theory is that put forward by Edgar Brightman who wondered if, in fact, God was not faced

[4] A fuller discussion of *das Nichtige* will be found on pages 132-150 of J. Hick's *Evil and the God of Love*, on which the above brief summary is based.

with conditions within His universe that finally resisted His will. Take for instance the Sahara desert or deformed babies. Have they any conceivable purpose? Are they dysteleological, having no 'end' or completion? If so, why does God allow them to be? Is it that He is faced with conditions that resist Him? It might be argued that these are First Order evils without which there cannot be certain Second Order goods, *e.g.* the lifelong love and devotion of the mother to the child. But that makes God seem monstrous! Can we defend Him by saying that He 'couldn't help it'. Well, I suppose one could, but then one would be no longer defending the sovereign God of the Bible. Besides, these 'conditions': are they 'outside' God (which is to admit dualism)? Or are they 'inside' God (in which case He is no longer 'good' as we understand the word)?

4. Another perhaps more biblical way of relieving God of the responsibility for the existence of evil is to blame it all on Satan in the first place and fallen angels in the second place.

These days it is unfashionable to believe in a personal devil, an actual leader of dark forces. But then it is unfashionable to believe in God as well and fashion does not alter fact. Jesus certainly regarded Satan as an individual; so did the New Testament writers. His name means 'adversary' or 'accuser' and in all his work he opposes God. A sinner himself, he tempts others to sin. He is the 'father of lies'; he is also the 'lord of death' and keeps men enslaved by their fear of death. Because of his violence and deceit Christians must be brave and watchful. He is the great counterfeiter who sows his servants among the faithful. He is sometimes called 'the ruler of this world'.

In the twentieth century it is not difficult to believe that Satan exists. Take any war, for instance the recent Nigerian conflict, with both 'sides' slowly polarizing and then with a diabolical logic locking in combat for more than two years, leaving two million dead and how many more fatherless and homeless. Is this really the work of man alone or has he been egged on to this orgy of self-destruction? Doubtless for a practical purpose the Christian will take the biblical view. It is healthy to be reminded that, with Paul and the rest, we are 'not contending against flesh and blood, but against the principalities, the powers, against the spiritual hosts of wickedness in the heavenly places'. There is a matter-of-fact reality about this Bible view which accords well with experience, not only in world affairs but in our own lives.

But having said all that, Satan will not do to resolve our problem. The most obvious and immediate question is, where did Satan come from? If he is a creature, then God made him and is still responsible. If God did not make him then we are back to dualism. If God made him, did He make him good or evil? We cannot say 'evil', so we guess He made him 'good'. How then did he become evil? Now there is great tradition on this point within Christendom, but the Bible is virtually silent. It seems to me therefore better to leave Satan out of it. I shall not, in the next chapter, seek to explain man's Fall in terms of Satan's temptation (*i.e.* assuming that the serpent of Genesis 3 is Satan): this would only push the problem one step back. We have so much more data about man, it would seem better to concentrate on his case without distraction. If in fact it is possible for 'evil' to arise 'spontaneously' without being positively created by God, then any position we might arrive at about man could presumably apply to any pre-history of Satan which is denied to us.

Solutions which deny statement 3

'Evils exist.' But who would deny such a statement?

1. Well, first and most obviously the Christian Scientists. One of their main beliefs is that all evil is illusory. It's 'all in

the mind' as a result of failing to think correctly about it. No-one would deny that there are many situations where such teaching is helpful: we advise a child 'to forget about it', when he has scratched his knee. Thinking about it makes it worse. Somebody condescends to us and we start brooding over an imaginary insult. Forget it! But the world's woe is worse than this. Are the thalidomide babies 'all in the mind'? Were the life-taking floods on the American east coast illusory?

The Christian rebuttal of this doctrine is perhaps to be found in the pains and death of Christ. The New Testament writers repeatedly emphasize that the evil and sin of the world was so real that it could be met only by the real death of an actual Son of God.

2. A more satisfying point of view is that of Spinoza who said that we only call an event 'evil' if we look at it from our own point of view. If only we could see the incident *sub specie aeternitatis* then we would see how it was necessary and part of the total good. If you go up close to a picture and look at the black triangle it does not look at all artistic or admirable. But stand back and see the picture as a whole and you will see that the black triangle is the shadow of the door half-open and that the picture, far from being improved by the removal of the 'black', would be ruined by it. Again we can see the truth in this idea in everyday life. Digging is hard work, weeding is tedious. So why bother? Stand back a bit and include the harvest in the picture and at once the toil is justified. This view of evil cannot be refuted, for if you say of a particular evil 'I cannot see how it fits in and enhances the picture' then the reply is 'Stand further back: you have not yet got a large enough view'. I suppose Spinoza would say that only God Himself can stand 'far enough back' to make sense of everything.

But the solution leaves us uneasy. There are *some* evils

which are just diabolical and the idea of God painting them in on the canvas for 'a bit of contrast' is horrifying. Surely He can paint better than that? Besides, to press the point, darkness may be merely the absence of light, but evil is much more than the absence of good. Evil is negative in the sense that it could not occur without the 'good', but it is very positive in the will which is pitted against God and which seeks to undo His work.

3. In the last hundred years or so there have arisen a number of theories which give what might be called the 'by-product' theory of evil, which in effect asserts that evil is illusory.

Take Marxism. Why is man jealous? Because goods are inequitably shared. Why does man fight? To regain what is rightfully his. Why are there wars? A result of some historical dialectic and man working in obedience to forces that he does not understand. Once the revolution has come and a true communistic state has been founded man will live with man in true brotherhood, in peace, in plenty and there will be no more struggle. Sin, evil, selfishness, *etc*. are the products of adverse economic situations. This is, of course, an over-simplification, but sin is regarded as a by-product of poverty. Bernard Shaw in *Pygmalion* makes Alfred Doolittle say, in reply to the question 'Have you no morals, man?': 'Can't afford them, Governor. Neither could you if you was as poor as me.'

I do not suppose that anyone holds such a naïve view today. Even in Communist states such as the USSR we still hear of men acting in an evil fashion. Joseph Stalin liquidated his opponents; civil servants in positions of trust turn them to private profit. Are these events really because of economic forces? Anyone who has lived between the ages of 20 and 30 can tell you that getting richer does *not* equal getting better.

Then there is the view held by some amateur psychologists that somehow psychology has demolished the notion of evil in man's make-up. A man who behaves badly is thought merely to be suffering from some kind of maladjustment, say a repression of his sexual drive. Or codes of behaviour are thought to be merely a collection of outdated conventions.

The true psychologist keeps to his psychological categories and by so doing cannot contradict a religious or moral account of man. Of course there are some psychoanalysts who are not Christian believers and sometimes give advice at variance with the Christian ethic. But they do this as philosophers not as scientists. The Christian psychoanalyst need not give up either his science or his Christianity.

The criminologist likewise is tempted to deny the existence of evil in the heart of man. Crime is sometimes said to be the result of poor housing, or broken homes, or the asphalt jungle. Poor upbringing or frustrated ambition produce social misfits. No-one, of course, would deny that these ghastly conditions do influence and magnify the evil in people. But does adverse environment produce evil in people? If it did then *all* the people reared in New York ghettoes or the slums of Liverpool would be delinquent: and they are not. Many rise 'above' their environment. Conversely, all those nicely brought up in congenial surroundings should be good people and yet they are not. From time to time there appears in the newspapers a confession from a criminal, that he had every chance as a young man, a good home, a good education and yet from perversity he 'went wrong'. Or was the wrong inside him all the time?

And then there are the people who keep out of the criminal courts. Are they good? They will say so only if they are self-deceived. Any law-abiding citizen can see in himself the same drives and impulses that unchecked have landed the criminal in trouble. But to keep out of prison is not the same as being 'good'. It used to be said in the army that the Good Conduct Medal was for '18 years of undetected crime'. It's only half a joke. You can keep out of the hangman's hands if you don't murder someone. But Jesus said if you are angry with your brother you will be liable to judgment.

Sociological theory also tends to have a by-product theory of evil. Professor Aron commenting on Marx says:[5]

> 'Marx not only distinguished infrastructure and superstructure; he also opposed social reality to consciousness. It is not men's consciousness that determines reality; on the contrary, it is the social reality that determines their consciousness. . . . Statements of this kind may provide a basis for what is referred to today as the sociology of knowledge.'

This kind of theory denies reality to 'ideologies' of law, politics, religion, ethics, aesthetics, philosophy. All these are mere rationalizations of the economic order of the forces and relations of production. If this is seriously accepted then the sociologists own 'ideology' of his theory is determined by 'social reality'. Any philosopher who places thinking and willing beneath some other 'reality' (e.g. 'matter' or 'economics') casts serious doubts on the validity of his own conclusions.

It would seem, then, that Christians *are* committed to asserting the three statements: that God is wholly good; that God is all-powerful; that evil exists. The solution I am about to put forward in the next chapter could be said to deny that 'God is all-powerful'. I shall argue that He *is* all-powerful, but in a crucial area deliberately limits His own power. He is able to do this because He can choose.

[5] *Main Currents in Sociological Thought,* I (Pelican Books, 1968), p. 123.

Do you think that evil and religion are (merely) psychological disorders?

Why should we take sides with 'good' in the matter of good and evil when so often evil seems to win? If you can't beat it, why not join it?

5 THE FREE WILL DEFENCE

The theodicy which I am prepared to put forward and defend is sometimes called the 'Free Will Defence', and I am going to dub it FWD. But first let me draw together certain conclusions I have reached in earlier chapters:

1 That moral evil has a flavour and an enmity towards God that natural evil does not have. Moral evil is by far the more serious of the two, both in quality and quantity.

2 The difficulty is that God is Creator and we have asserted He has unlimited power. He is responsible, therefore, in an ultimate sense even for the rebellion of man.

3 That there is a valid distinction to be made between First and Second Order approval. But for it to be valid for God Himself, we must be able to agree that man has freedom.

FWD

Let me state the defence. According to the New Testament, 'God is good'. But this is not the main category used: it would be better to say 'God is loving', deliberately using a verb rather than an adjective.

Everything that He made, He loved. The New Testament word that is used, *agapē*, does not take its meaning from its roots but from its use. The *locus classicus* is 1 John 4, where *agapē* is closely connected with the self-giving of

Christ on the cross. Christian *agapē* is particularly characterized by being other-centred. Friendship-love, married-love, family-love often contain an element of self-centredness. But *agapē* cares only for the one loved.

It can be seen, then, that only God is pure *agapē* because for Him to love Himself seems to imply a choice between Himself and His creation, and that is unthinkable. Indeed that impossible question 'Why did God create at all?' might conceivably receive an answer in the statement 'God is *agapē*'. Loving and creating are both outwardgoing activities.

So He created: the 'stuff' itself, monomers and polymers, inorganic, vegetation, fishes, birds, mammals, vertebrates and invertebrates, reptiles and insects. How He did it, we may leave the scientists to investigate. All that need concern us here is that *He* did it. But where should He finish? The matter could not be complete until He made a creature that could return His *agapē*.

The pangs of unrequited love most of us know. But it must be nothing to the 'pang' of there being no-one existent and capable of returning love. This is to speak anthropomorphically of course, but there is a certain logic about it. So God created man 'in his own image' with the ability to understand, the ability to choose and the ability to love. These three are closely connected. When I talk of 'understanding a person' I mean a great deal more than the fact that we know the same language or use a common vocabulary. If I choose, this presupposes understanding, and if I love, this presupposes choosing. That man is marked off from the rest of creation is obvious. Among many peoples in scattered parts of Africa[1] it is narrated that man came from heaven or another world. The Bachwa Pygmies in the Congo call themselves 'the children of God':

[1] John Mbiti, *African Religions and Philosophy* (Heinemann, 1969).

Scripture says that God made man in His own image.

Without the freedom to choose, there can be no true love. If I can coerce the beloved then I cannot fairly claim to be loved back. Even with a dog, I cannot claim that it is well trained unless the leash is off. Assuming for a moment, then, that it is possible, God let man off the leash and gave him autonomy.

What happens next is that man exercises his choosing. He places himself instead of God at the centre, perhaps only momentarily, but it is enough. Man the supreme creation exercises his supreme ability, to be free and to love, to commit the supreme evil – rebellion against the Creator. The rest of the animals could never understand or be involved in the same way, for this is self-conscious and deliberate. All moral evil stems from this moment.

But immediately we cry 'But didn't God *know* this would happen?' and we are answered 'Yes: God knows all things'. Then why should He have created man free? We are on dangerous ground when we speculate on God's state of mind before creation, but one thing seems to be clear: the conditions for having loving beings are exactly the same as the conditions for having rebellious beings. God is all-powerful but that does not mean that He can do anything. He cannot make $2+2=5$ and He cannot make it raining and not-raining at the same moment in the same place. These are not, as some have argued, limitations on God's power as though some Platonic arithmetic were forcing its will on to Him. It is simply that He is rational. In one of G. K. Chesterton's 'Father Brown' stories, a crook masquerading as a priest airily suggests that perhaps God is above and beyond reason. He is speedily unmasked by that Catholic detective, who well knows that no priest would talk such nonsense. When we say God is all-powerful we mean He can do all things that can be done which doubtless includes many things that are impossible to man. But we do not mean that He can give a hydrogen atom and a helium atom the same atomic structure. Even God could not create free men without at the same time creating men who were able to rebel.

Now the FWD has come under heavy attack both by Christian and non-Christian philosophers. But before I try to meet those attacks I want to set out the reasons why I believe that man was originally free and why he is still, occasionally, free.

1 The Bible's doctrine of judgment

I have already referred to the Christian doctrine of God as Judge. Take the Ten Commandments; they are given to us assuming that we can do something about it. Take the Sermon on the Mount; it concludes with a parabolic warning that if we listen and do nothing about it, we shall be like a foolish man building his house on a foundation of sand. The point of the parable is to encourage us to 'build on the rock', that is to listen to Jesus' words and act upon them. Near the end of His ministry Jesus told a whole series of parables: about the foolish and wise bridesmaids; about the industrious and slothful servants; about the shameful tenants who tried to usurp their master's property; about the sheep and the goats. And all these parables are shouting at us:

> It *does* matter how you behave.
> There *is* a judgment or crisis which you must face.
> You *can* change your ways and your attitudes.
> You *can* be saved and commended rather than lost or rejected.

Paul goes even further. Despite his strong doctrine of salvation and the blessedness of the saved he asserts in warning to the Corinthian church, 'we must *all* appear before the judgment seat of Christ, so that each one may receive good or evil, according to what he has done in the body'.

Now this teaching about judgment is not confined to one or two proof texts: it runs throughout the whole standpoint of the Bible. To me this can mean only one thing: that man is responsible for his actions, otherwise judgment would become a farce. And we are only 'responsible' when we could have acted otherwise; that is, we were free to choose and we chose wrongly.

2 Kant and the idea of 'ought'

In his moral theory Kant laid great emphasis on that distinctively moral feeling we have when we say 'I ought . . .'. I have in fact been rude to old Snodgrass; but 'I *ought* to have treated him gently'. The moment I say 'I ought' I am aware that I was free to behave differently. I cannot argue my 'ought' from observable facts: all I can see is what I actually did. But it was wrong. 'I *ought*' to have done the opposite. This idea comes plunging into my mind from nowhere, but it is urgent and compelling. The voice of conscience, the voice of God, call it what you will, but when you hear it you know you are free to choose.

This faculty of self-criticism that man has is remarkable. (It has analogies in animal behaviour, as when my dog appears to hesitate in eating meat off the table; in fact he is balancing two fears – fear of being beaten and fear of losing a tasty bit. But if the dog succeeds in taking the meat there is no remorse afterwards.) What is particularly remarkable about conscience is that it should continue to exist at all when so often we ignore its recommendations. It was the same with the Hebrew prophets; no-one took any notice of them at the time but somehow their oracles survived to be included in the sacred canon, only to be ignored again in Jesus' day.

My explanation of this as a Christian is that both conscience and the prophets were given by God to remind us of the ways of love. John the Baptist used to speak to Herod of his sin and Herod liked to listen. Finally Herod chopped his head off. We are like that; glad to have a conscience but reluctant to obey it. It testifies to us that we are free to choose. 'Ought' implies 'can'.

3 The fabric of everyday life

Now it may be philosophically argued that this freedom I experience is an illusion. What is very plain from the Bible is that if it is an 'illusion', then it is one on which it is right and proper for us to act. And this is also plain from everyday life. All society, law courts, schoolmasters, parents and all in authority take freedom as a foundation for their *modus operandi*. If I turn up late at a party and explain to my hostess that I have been ensnared by a mechanistic universe she will give me an odd look. But if I commit murder and tell the judge that I am merely a collection of biochemical reactions and that he is another such collection, I will soon find myself between a mere four walls. Or if I cripple my child in a fit of rage and tell the NSPCC that 'it is God's will because He is responsible for all His creation', I deserve to be branded as a monster.

Everywhere men are generally held to be responsible for their actions and there is no satisfactory practical alternative. If freedom is an illusion, then this is very odd. Philosophy is concerned with truth and not argument. If the philosophers can show us the truth on which to mould society let us abandon our illusion of freedom and use their truth instead. But they cannot and there is none. How pathetic are those attempts that would construe all wrong-doing as a kind of disease for which there is, somewhere, a scientific treatment. The man who believes *that* must be a stranger to the secrets of his own heart.

But God made man . . .

But why could not God have made free beings who would in fact have chosen what is right and loving? Perhaps if God knew as He was about to create A that A would rebel against Him, why should He then not leave A and go on to B?

J. Hick has two radical criticisms to make in respect of this account of freedom and fall. Here is the first:

> 'The notion that man was at first spiritually and morally good, orientated in love towards his Maker, and free to express his flawless nature without even the hindrance of contrary temptations, and yet that he preferred to be evil and miserable, cannot be saved from the charge of self-contradiction and absurdity.'[2]

There are two things to be said in reply. First, the phrase 'he preferred to be evil' may be deliberately paradoxical, but I suspect that it is in fact merely inviting us to think of the Fall as absurd. You cannot 'prefer evil' simply because 'evil' in normal usage is 'what I disapprove and shrink from.' The assumption is that Adam *knew* that he was about to be evil and miserable, and gladly chose it. I agree that this would be absurd. But I am not at all sure that the choice for Adam was between good and evil, between happiness and misery. It seems to me to be an important point that the forbidden fruit came from the Tree of the Knowledge of Good and Evil, which implies that Adam

---

[2] *Evil and the God of Love*, p. 75.

did not *know* what good and evil were until he had made the fatal mistake.

Then what did he choose between, if he didn't know good and evil? He chose between God and himself. God said one thing and he thought another and he decided in favour of himself. This is the only naked choice open to someone who is innocent and capable of love; but to say that Adam was innocent does not mean that he was omniscient.

I have heard it said that the forbidden tree was placed in the garden as 'the gateway to moral maturity'. I disagree. If Adam had never sinned, he would never have known good or evil, he would never have known morality and *he would have been better off*. The Fall is what it says, a step down – not a step towards maturity. It would be a poor defence for a man determined on a licentious life to say 'but I will get more knowledge and knowledge is good'. Some things are better left unknown.

The decision that Adam faced has some analogy even in these times. Suppose I am trying to convert an atheist friend. If I could clearly set before him heaven and hell and ask him to choose, he must choose heaven. But the choice, as he sees it, is not like this. The choices he makes are: deciding between reading a book on Christian truth and reading a new book in his subject that has just been published; deciding between losing the friendship of *x* and *y* and joining a miserable, introverted society called the church; deciding between a life of discipline under authority and a life of civilized hedonism. In every case the path to hell is paved with decisions that are natural.

The second thing I would want to say in reply to the quotation from Hick is this. The two key phrases in the quotation are 'orientated in love' and 'flawless nature'. Now these expressions imply a theory about choice and will to which I do not think it is necessary to subscribe. To make this theory clear, may I quote again:

> 'Augustine's conception of our human freedom is identical with that of a number of contemporary philosophers who define a free act as one that is not externally compelled but that flows from the nature and will of the agent.'[3]

I certainly agree that external compulsion denies freedom, but what is here asserted is that freedom comes from an internal compulsion. Man must not be thought to be random or unpredictable. There is of course a truth in this: our characters, that is the *psyche* plus innumerable small decisions, do greatly influence how we choose. People often are predictable, and if they were not life would lose a lot of spice. But it is a two-way affair. The decisions make the character as well as the character influencing the decisions. If we could never choose absolutely then we could never change our characters. Again in Hick's words, 'a man's actions are determined by his own inner nature'. The deeper criticism of FWD is now apparent: if God made us and therefore made our natures, why could He not make those natures to issue in actions which always resulted in *agapē*? We would still be 'free' because the action would flow from our 'flawless nature' but we would always choose God rather than self because we would be 'orientated in love'. Determinism has been smuggled in because 'free' now means 'determined in their nature by God'.

All theories of the will that appeal to motive tend to destroy the notion of freedom. Of course in assessing the *value* of an action one will take into account the motive, *i.e.* the state of mind of the agent while he was acting. But to suggest that the motive somehow *moves* (as the etymology

³ *Ibid.*, p. 74.

suggests) the agent to action denies that he is active; he is not active, he is passive following his genes and environment. All I wish to assert when I say that man was given freedom is to say that he is able to choose between two people or courses of action. Supposing a man is about to make an important decision such as changing his job. Before he decides he may do a number of things: he draws up a list of pros and cons, he consults his friends, he asks his wife. As time passes he begins to perceive that some factors are more important than others and these will finally influence his decision. But notice how misleading these passive expressions in the previous sentence are. Who decides which factors are important? Who chooses the friends to whom he goes for advice? Who decides which advice is better than another? It is true that by the time he comes to make his formal decision, he may have taken his decision earlier. But who decided that his wife's peace of mind should come before everything else? If he had to choose between two motives, say the desire to get rich and the desire to live away from London, who is to tell him which is the most important? In the last analysis all we can say is, he decided. In the words of G. E. Moore in another context, choice is 'simple and unanalysable'.

Hick quotes Schleiermacher with approval: 'The more perfect these good angels are supposed to have been, the less possible it is to find any motive but those presupposing a fall already, *e.g.* arrogance and envy.' Notice that motive is appealed to as a cause of choice. But when I choose between two people I do not have a 'motive' in the classic sense: I just choose.

Perhaps the most naked example of choice is when I have to choose between two people. To which do I give my loyalty? It is at moments like this when I come nearest to that primal choice of Adam's.

It is in the New Testament garden of Gethsemane that

we see the reverse of Adam. The final hurdle was 'Not my will, but thine, be done :[4] a naked decision between self and God. It is not for nothing that Paul says becoming a Christian is like getting married.[5] Jesus said 'Deny yourself and follow me':[6] there is the plain choice all of us face at some time.

Hick's second radical criticism of the Free Will Defence is this:

> 'It would be hard to clear God from ultimate responsibility for the existence of sin in view of the fact that He chose to create a being whom He foresaw would, if He created him, freely sin.'[7]

I am not at all sure that I want to clear God from responsibility nor that He would want me to. If I have succeeded in the FWD, then it does make sense to talk of God's First and Second Order Approval. When I commit sin, for instance by failing to feed a hungry person, God gives me His First Order Approval by holding my molecules together. He wills me, a free person to exist. But in so far as He has created a substance 'like' Himself He withholds His Second Order or moral Approval of my action. To use an old-fashioned but usable distinction, He is immanent in my physical existence but transcendent in His judgment of my sin. I suppose He could withdraw His First Order approval whenever He saw me about to incur His Second Order disapproval but then life as we know it would simply cease to exist.

God is, of course, ultimately responsible for His creation. But whether this means I should 'blame' Him is another matter. We may sometimes *feel* like blaming Him as in Sydney Carter's song:

[4] Luke 22:42.   [5] Ephesians 5:21-33.   [6] Luke 9:23.
[7] Ibid., p. 75.

'It's God they ought to crucify
Instead of you and me.'

To say He is not responsible is to deny Christian orthodoxy
and adopt instead some form of dualism. In this chapter I
have tried to show that the existence of moral evil is not
inconsistent with a loving Creator. Whether this is satisfactory or not will also depend on the purpose of it all.
This I shall discuss later in chapter 10.

QUESTIONS FOR FURTHER THOUGHT AND DISCUSSION

If a man is not free, why do we punish people?

Where does 'conscience' come from? If man is a 'whole'
why should he criticize himself when 'wrong' acts are often
to his advantage?

Can you reconcile the different views of man held by the
biochemist and the probation officer?

6 THE PROBLEM OF FREEDOM

In this chapter I shall attempt to discuss or meet some of the objections which might be raised against what has been said so far.

1 Man is not free because he lives in a mechanistic world

The argument is this. All the things around me are governed by laws. Some of these laws have been discovered, some still await discovery. But, given time, science will have a complete description of man's environment, how it interlocks and acts. Man cannot be thought of as acting freely in such a context.

Professor Gilbert Ryle in his book *The Concept of Mind* points out that the physical world may *govern* everything I do but that it *ordains* nothing. He uses an example of the billiard table: once the cue-ball has been struck everything is governed by coefficients, of restitution and the like. But they do not ordain how I strike the cue-ball nor do they decide whether I should strike it or not.

Furthermore, unless we live in a rigid mechanistic world there is no scope for wisdom, folly, skill, love, *etc*. For if I decided to do something, say shoot at goal, and then half way the ball went off in a hyperbolic arc without any cause, then it would not matter if I were a skilful footballer or not. All would have equal chance of scoring in a variable world.

Similarly there would be no recognizable right or wrong, love or hate as it would be impossible to tell by inspection what kind of action was intended.

2 Man is not free because he himself is a mechanism

Physiologists and biochemists are continually doing research using the phrase 'man is a mechanism' as their first principle. They get results: it is a very usable tool. But 'man is not free because he himself is a mechanism' is one of those statements which conceal a 'merely'. Is that all he is? Certainly not! You can dissect a man on the table and never discover his liking for mushrooms nor his taste for metaphysics.

But, it may be argued, one day scientists will be able to give an exhaustive account of the psychophysiological changes in the human brain. Then it will be seen that man's decisions are completely predictable and therefore he cannot be free to choose. It does not follow. A complete description of the brain at the moment of choosing no more removes the category of decision than a complete description of light waves from an oil-painting removes the category of beauty.[1]

3 Man is not free because God fixes everything

This theological objection is sometimes made by Christians but more often by those who know that 'predestination' is a knotty problem. Whole books have been written on this, so I can hardly cover the subject in a brace of paragraphs.

A thorough examination of the Bible usually finishes up with two apparently irreconcilable statements:

[1] See Donald M. Mackay, *The Clockwork Image* (Inter-Varsity Press, 1974), pp. 78 ff. on 'Responsibility' and 'Predestination'.

1 Man is responsible for his actions.
2 God orders or ordains all things.

It can be argued convincingly that God's foreknowledge does not affect my freedom. Knowledge is subsequent to the thing known logically, though chronologically it may precede it. If I predict that the light leaving the sun now will reach me in $8\frac{1}{2}$ minutes then the event, the light actually arriving, makes the prediction a piece of knowledge. If some catastrophic event prevented the arrival of the light then the knowledge vanishes.

But it is doubtful if one can make the distinction for God. What difference is there for Him in knowing and willing? After all He only has to think something and it is! His thoughts do not have the airy, dreamy quality of the ideas which flit through our heads. They are intolerably solid, like the world around us, like our own bodies. 'Who is John Robinson?' asked Michael Flanders. 'Just an idea in the mind of God.' Notice that word 'just'! An Idea in the mind of God should have at least a capital letter.

When I say 'God fixes everything' I may be saying no more than that He extends His First Order Approval to all that exists. It does not settle the argument as to whether He has, in fact, created beings in His 'image' with power to choose.

We are treading on holy ground: struggling to see into the mind of God, boldly applying our own puny introspection to discover His thought-processes. These statements 1 and 2 above cannot perhaps be systematized: but they can be put to wrong uses. Some theologians have said, 'Since 2 is true, there is no need, indeed no possibility, of repentance, unless of course God gives it'. They have expounded one Scripture to be contrary to another. 'Ah,' says the sceptic, 'that's what I've always said. The Bible is full of contradictions.' This all depends on how you use and interpret the Scriptures. On a practical level there is no difficulty.

'Follow me!² Repent and believe in the gospel',³ says Jesus. We do, and then He says, 'You have not chosen me, but I have chosen you.'⁴ Is He now contradicting himself? No! He is encouraging us to understand that our Christian fruitfulness is based on His decision, not merely on a decision of our own. Whenever one of these statements is held to the exclusion of the other, the person concerned is no longer following what Jesus actually said.

4 God could have created man free so that in fact he always chose right

This is Professor Antony Flew's argument with which he claims to have broken the back of the FWD.⁵ Using the paradigm case of the smiling bridegroom he infers that 'there is no contradiction involved in saying that a particular action or choice was: both *free*, and could have been helped; and *predictable* . . . and explicable in terms of caused causes'. He expresses some doubt as to whether this sort of argument is sound. And Professor Ernest Gellner in his book *Words and Things* (pp. 33-40), accepting for a moment Flew's conclusion then goes on, 'Furthermore . . . omnipotence might have . . . created people who would always as a matter of fact freely have chosen to do the right thing.' Now this simply does not follow. If men are in fact free, then their acts come first and logically accurate prediction comes second. That men are not free is assumed by Flew who implies that men's acts could somehow be determined by God, that man could be 'programmed' to act rightly.

It has been further argued that if man is 'off the leash' then some part of God's creation is out of control which is precisely what the doctrine of creation denies. It is true that

² Mark 2:14. ³ Mark 1:15. ⁴ John 15:16, AV.
⁵ *New Essays in Philosophical Theology* (SCM, 1955), pp. 144-169.

in the 'nature' Psalms (*e.g.* Psalms 93, 104) the whole of nature is seen to be under God's control, but the biblical descriptions of sinful man, the opposition of the demons to Jesus' work and, supremely, the death of Jesus on the cross sound as though things were at least temporarily 'out of control'; never finally, of course, for all things must have God's First Order Approval. The doctrinal counterpart of this loss of control is the eschatological triumph over the powers of evil, within man or outside him, of which Jesus's ministry was a foretaste.

5 Couldn't God have arranged things better?

This kind of objection is usually raised after the recitation of a long catalogue of ills which give some idea of the vast cumulative suffering in the world. Start with the last war and add all the displaced persons, unemployment, cancer, thalidomide babies, oppression by tyrants, victims of the economic rat-race, earthquakes, hurricanes, race wars, mental suffering, communist infiltration, assassination, brain-washing and you might well ask, 'Couldn't God have arranged things better?' It puts the Christian in a cleft stick. If he says 'yes' it sounds as though he admits himself to be better than God. But if he says 'no' he makes God sound like a cosmic torturer.

There is first a preliminary point which has been made by C. S. Lewis that it is misleading to talk of the 'sum of human misery'. Each man has to bear his own pain and misery but not everybody else's as well. No-one (except possibly God Himself) has to bear the composite pain. Supposing a man fails his examination; his disappointment is hardly increased by knowing he is in a large company. It is true that we have a vague sympathy with the suffering millions, but if I were called on to *feel* their anguish I should be in a mental hospital within a week. Flew calls this argument 'a desperate manoeuvre' but again has recourse only to ordinary language usage and admits that we cannot do an impossible piece of applied arithmetic.

But I would like to argue that our present world-system is not an 'arrangement' at all; if God is God there must be an element of necessity in the creation. If God must have free men, then He must also have the conditions which can produce the present chaos. If the cricketer wants to be able to hit the ball he must also logically be able to hit the wicket-keeper. Is this really 'the best of all possible worlds'? If may be possible to suggest improvements here and there, e.g. why shouldn't man only live to the age of 30, or why should there be any metal ores in the earth's crust (without them there would be little technology and virtually no communication and perhaps less suffering)? But we would still be left with moral evil which is the greatest source of suffering.

Without falling into the medieval trap of equating 'being' with 'goodness', the Christian feels that God has not made a mistake. If God is the author, what is must be. If the result looks pretty poor to us, we are perhaps only saying how little we understand the logical outworking of rebellion.

6 The FWD has nothing to say about 'natural' evil

The disease-death environment

I have already argued that death, as part of the animal environment, need not necessarily be linked with the Fall of man. I think, however, that it is possible that disease may be. The emphasis in the curse in Genesis 3 is on added pain (pain itself must have already existed in a mechanistic world). There are one or two hints[6] in the New Testament

[6] E.g. Luke 13:16.

that Satan (*i.e.* moral evil) is somehow involved with disease. And Jesus' ministry of salvation was to the '*whole* man', a phrase that recurs to show that Jesus fought sin and disease on much the same terms. We instinctively feel that God is on the side of doctors and nurses. This would imply that a child with polio, whom we discussed earlier, is not suffering because God decides it but because it is another part of his creation 'out of control'. In the person of Jesus, disease is fought and overcome; all His disciples and those who heal today are doing 'His work'.

The evil effects of death are elusive to define. We all fear death primarily because we do not know what lies beyond. Those who believe in God and 'know' Him simply do not fear death in the same way. If appearances mean anything, countless martyrs of many nations have died serene. The phrase 'better dead than red' testifies to the fact that men do not regard death as the ultimate tragedy; there are personal betrayals which are worse.

There are some interesting words of Jesus in Luke 13:4, 5:

> 'Those eighteen upon whom the tower in Siloam fell and killed them, do you think that they were worse offenders than all the others who dwelt in Jerusalem? I tell you, No; but unless you repent you will all likewise perish.'

Jesus denies that a particular 'violent' death is a particular judgment on an individual, but the violent event is a reminder that we are all under judgment. If you read in the paper that 150 people have died in a train-crash, the Christian reaction is not to point the finger, but to repent. It will be our turn all too soon.

This is the most beneficial effect that the disease-death environment has on us. It reminds us, day in, day out, that 'this world is not my home'. There is no doubt that most of us are spiritually lazy; that very few of us are like Abraham who 'went out, not knowing where he was to go . . . For he looked forward to the city which has foundations, whose builder and maker is God'.[7] The worry of pain and the tear of death are like goads which save us from the complacency which would be content with second best. As long as man remains as he is, a world without pain, disappointments, obstructions and frustrations might well lead to such an increase of arrogance and hardness of heart that life would become insupportable. The world as it is appears to be the only suitable home for man as he is. The tearless world of heaven is a suitable home for man as he will be.

Natural catastrophies

Increase of speed in communication in these days means that as soon as a great disaster occurs we hear about it. Our newspapers are full of bad news about earthquakes, cyclones, tidal waves, and drought; events which leave a trail of human misery in their wake. Is this the best that God can do? After all He made this environment in which we live; could He not have done better? Why does He allow natural events to be so hostile to man? Can it be argued that these natural disasters are a result of sin?

In the Bible catastrophies are sometimes, as in the case of Sodom, forecast as the judgment of God and therefore a 'result' of sin. But it would not be right always so to construe them. Poor harvests are mentioned in Genesis 41 in the story of Joseph and in Acts 11 when Agabus foretold a 'great famine'. In neither case are these famines regarded as a punishment for sin. And yet I believe that human suffering from natural disaster is an indirect result of man being out of touch with God.

[7] Hebrews 11:8, 10.

Some parts of the world are more hazardous to live in than others. If you live on the banks of a river; on the slope of a volcano or a mountain covered with snow; in an area of low or uncertain rainfall; astride a major tectonic line: then you may expect floods, eruptions, avalanches, drought and earthquakes. How is it that man has come to live in such inhospitable areas? It is immediately interesting to note that the environment provided by God for Adam was hospitable (even thistles were prohibited!) and that, because of his disobedience, Adam was driven out into an inhospitable region where life was much tougher.

There then followed a series of migrations from the Mesopotamian basin which anthropologists agree to be the starting-point for all races of *homo sapiens* existent on earth today. One of these ancient migrations is referred to in Genesis 11 in the story of Babel. It says 'the Lord scattered them abroad over the face of all the earth' and the record suggests that this scattering was a result of false worship and human pride. No doubt through ignorance of climate and the nature of the earth's crust many of these people settled in inhospitable areas. The point is that such settlements were made as a result of disregarding God.

Later, in the second millenium BC, God directed the migration of Abraham and his family. An integral part of the promise was an hospitable area to live in, a 'land flowing with milk and honey'. Amos, the prophet, refers to other migrations directed by God, but this does not mean that *all* migrations were His will. Sometimes migration was caused by hostility and aggression;[8] sometimes by man spoiling an area by over-grazing or de-forestation; some-

---

[8] It is quite wrong to interpret the Israelite migration from Egypt to Canaan as the result of aggression following a desire for territorial aggrandizement. The Bible writers make it clear that the justification for the invasion was judgment on the corrupt society of the original inhabitants. This was also the reason for the *removal* of the Israelites from the land 600 years later (see 2 Kings 21:9-15).

times just in search of 'living-room'. Did men *have* to live in inhospitable areas? Before the arrival of modern medicine and the population explosion the answer was No.

Most people now live where they do, however, because they were born there. They cannot, except in a few adventurous cases, go and live somewhere else. This does not mean that you can blame God. If your great . . . grandparents were selfish or foolish or lazy in choosing an environment or a life-pattern which is precarious, then you will suffer (innocently, no doubt) as you are involved in the consequences of that decision. The sins of the fathers can be visited on the children long past the fourth generation.

And what about the sins of our own generation? 'Pollution' has now become a fashionable word. But the desecration of the environment which it represents has been going on for centuries. We are now past the cheerful optimism that believes that all machines, drugs and inventions are beneficial because of their pleasant short-term effects. Our technology and greed have far outstripped our wisdom and forethought. One of the reasons for this is that we are out of touch with God. In the famines referred to above (in Genesis 41 and Acts 11) God sent His prophets to warn the people to take action, action which otherwise they could not have taken because of ignorance.

The problems which faced our migrating ancestors and which face us today have an element in common: ignorance. How could a migrating Bantu tribesman avoid the western rift valley because it is a seismic area? He could not: he was ignorant. And we are ignorant. It is now becoming apparent how little we know about ecology, geology, biochemistry, sociology. We are not in a position to make soundly based decisions which will be effective in the long term. A few years ago a campaigning politician in Britain was promising the electorate a 'scientifically planned economy'. We never got it: we simply do not know enough about economics. And if someone does come up with a good idea like the United Nations or artificial birth-control its implementation and effect are distorted and diluted by selfishness, sectional interests, prejudice and obscurantism. But, it may be argued, ignorance is not a sin. I am not so sure. It can be a sin and in the first place was the result of sin when man cut himself off from the source of all wisdom.

We tend to blame God for natural catastrophies but against this I would argue first, that there is no evidence that God wished us to populate inhospitable areas in the first place. Secondly, that the inhospitable areas have been populated as the result of going away from God and making poor decisions in ignorance. Thirdly, that both ancient and modern man has spoiled and polluted the hospitable areas and is in a poor position to criticize God's provision of environment.

One more point. It is certain that human sin greatly amplifies these evils and that human compassion vastly mitigates the misery caused by them. The mariner fears the storm and the rocks, but he fears the wreckers more. A man's house may be flooded out, but the love and help of his neighbours may break down barriers of reserve and selfishness which have been crippling him for years.

Nor is natural disaster the 'problem' for most people that moral disaster is. People are extraordinarily 'philosophical' (meaning they are *not*!) about natural calamities. These are just accepted as part of nature, something to be fought and overcome. If I am walking up a mountain and a rock falls and injures my foot, that's 'bad luck'. If an identical injury is done to me through a badly built wall collapsing I feel resentment at the builder. But if the same hurt is caused by my enemy hurling a stone at me I am furious and plot revenge. Often it is not the injury that is evil, but the context and the attitude of the injured.

This is superbly expressed in 2 Corinthians 7:10 (NEB):

> 'The wound which is borne in God's way brings a
> change of heart too salutary to regret; but the hurt
> which is borne in the world's way brings death.'

Animal pain

Why should God have instituted a system where life can
be supported only at the expense of life? Is this the best He
can do?

An obvious distinction can be made between plant life
and sentient animal life. The life of plants is necessary to
synthesize the polymers which are the bricks for more
complex organisms. A further distinction can be made
between conscious animals and self-conscious man. A large
measure of the fear and distress that I feel in the presence of
pain or death is a product of imagination or knowledge
which animals show no sign of possessing. The dentist's
waiting-room is sometimes worse than his chair.

If observations mean anything, then animals do not have
these general fears. I have seen a film showing hartebeeste
grazing 40 yards away from a lion busy consuming another
hartebeeste. No human parallel is conceivable. Animals
seem to live in the present and are unaffected by neuroses.
The trouble is that we all project our feelings into animals,
especially into pet animals. We thus suffer for them what
they never feel themselves. How do I know? Well, of
course, I don't know and because of this the argument will
never be settled. But while there is something very reasonable in the RSPCA trying to prevent cruelty to animals by
people, there would be something very absurd in raising
funds to protect rabbits from foxes, or mayflies from
swallows.

The suggestion has been made that the animal world is

the 'best', because it is a living demonstration of the 'terrible aspect' of God's love. Love involves sacrifice and suffering. 'Greater love has no man than this, to lay down his life for his friends.' Love involves surrender. Thus we are invited to see each animal death as one individual surrendering its life so that another life may continue. I have several objections to this.

First, the animal flying in fear, doing all it can to shake off pursuit, does not remotely look like a willing surrender. Second, it is difficult to see what *purpose* such a system could have. To tell us about the nature of God's love? But we would never have guessed that He was love at all from observation of nature. God is *not* empirically observable in the universe, otherwise we could compel faith. Third, this notion is closely associated by G. MacGregor[9] with the moral evolutionary view of creation. He argues that what we see in the animals is some kind of primitive moral decision. His position is based on the view that there are no gaps in nature and that in some sense the whole universe is moral. But the biblical account of creation says there *is* a gap in nature, that man is distinct from the rest. And *only* man is moral, only man has eaten of the tree of knowledge of good and evil.

A more satisfying speculation is that after the animal creation had been created there was demonic intervention by fallen angels, who had chosen wrongly in another sphere before the Fall of man. This satanic power corrupted the animals, or some of them, so that they lived by destroying others. The theory has a very slender biblical support based on hints rather than assertions. Its advantage is that it brands carnivorousness with the mark of moral evil. The main objection is that the whole of 'nature' is too far removed from God. Is the butterfly incorrupt and the mosquito an emissary of Satan? The psalmist speaks of

[9] *Introduction to Religious Philosophy* (Macmillan, 1960), chapter 39.

God giving the young lions their meat (Psalm 104:21) and in the command after the flood God says 'Every moving thing that lives shall be food for you' (Genesis 9:3). Surely if eating the flesh of animals is the work of Satan, Jesus would have been a vegetarian!

My own speculation on the matter is that the vegetable and animal world provide a superb backcloth to the uniqueness of man. 'Nature' is governed by the principle of the survival of the fittest and strongest. Man, if Jesus is right, is intended to live by the survival of the humblest. (See Luke 14:11: 'he who humbles himself will be exalted'.) Man-at-his-worst follows the animal principle and we get war, exploitation, *laissez-faire* economics, redundancy and mental homes full of 'failures'. But man-at-his-best lavishes care on the weak, subordinates himself to the interests of others, works hard and selflessly; in a word, he loves. Being great in the kingdom of heaven is very different from being great in the world or the animal kingdom. 'Whoever would be first among you must be slave of all' (Mark 10:44). Jesus lived by this principle. And, of course, they killed Him. Natural selection dismissed Him.

It might be objected to this solution that God caused a lot of suffering just to paint a backcloth. But against this I would argue as follows: first, I do not believe that suffering in nature has any of the connotations it has for us. I would quote Hick in support: 'the picture of animal life as a dark ocean of agonizing fear and pain is quite gratuitous'.[10] Second, we have a clear statement in Romans 8:19-21 that God having 'subjected' nature will finally set it free:

> 'For the creation waits with eager longing for the revealing of the sons of God; for the creation was subjected to futility, not of its own will but by the will of him who subjected it in hope; because the creation

10 *Evil and the God of Love*, pp. 346-350.

itself will be set free from its bondage to decay and obtain the glorious liberty of the children of God.'

This passage maintains the biblical emphasis that the creation is primarily centred on God and secondarily on man, the crown of creation. He is already in the image of God, but must become a son of God. He can only do this by 'receiving Christ'. He must learn his lesson, not from below, from the birds and the bees as evolutionary theologians imply, but from above, from Christ, the Son Himself. Then when he has been set free, the rest of creation can follow suit. Carnivorousness will cease and the lion will lie down with the lamb (see Isaiah 11:6-9).

QUESTIONS FOR FURTHER THOUGHT AND DISCUSSION

Do you really think that, as science advances, man's freedom of will will be seen to be an illusion?

If an avalanche overwhelms (a) an Alpine village, (b) a mountaineer in winter, is there any difference between the two situations as to whether the event is 'evil'?

Christ preached 'survival of the humblest'. Which would you prefer (to share a flat with) – someone who *lived* by this principle or someone who *lived* by 'survival of the fittest'?

7 GOD'S FINAL DEFEAT?

The Free Will Defence looks backward in an attempt to justify how evil arose in a universe created by a good and powerful God. But if the entrance of evil is a puzzle, the exit of evil is even more difficult, if indeed the free will God has given to man is absolute. If a man is really free then, logically, he may finally refuse to put his faith in God, he may refuse to obey His commandments, in other words he may refuse to 'enter the kingdom of God'; he is outside. Now if he is outside, then somewhere in God's creation there is an area of influence which is not 'under control'; and while this may be possible temporarily, can this situation exist perpetually? What can God do with the human soul who finally resists His demands, His commands, His love?

There seems to be only three possibilities: first, the rebel under pressure from the divine love changes his mind and enters the kingdom; or, second, the rebel is annihilated; or, third, the rebel is condemned to an eternal hell.

Universalism

The first possibility is by far the most attractive from the point of view of the theodicist. As I shall argue later (in chapter 10) the only final justification for the existence of evil is that it is finally the means to a good. If there are some souls who are finally outside God's 'plan', either destroyed or in hell, then their evil is an unmitigated, unredeemed evil and serves no useful purpose whatsoever in God's creation. The old scholastic argument that somehow the sufferings of those in hell improve the felicity of those in heaven is rejected no matter how delicately such an argument may be put. So if salvation is universal and all shall be saved, all the moral evil of the creation will have a good end. (Some have even thought that the devil himself could be redeemed.)

It is possible to adduce some support for this view from the New Testament: Paul, writing to Timothy, speaks of '. . . God our Saviour, who desires all men to be saved and to come to the knowledge of the truth'; and writing to the Philippians, '. . . at the name of Jesus every name should bow, . . . and every tongue confess that Jesus Christ is Lord . . .'.[1] I do not think that the universalistic interpretation is the right way of reading these verses, but it must be admitted that it is a possible interpretation. What is so difficult for this point of view is what to do with the surprisingly large number of sayings from Jesus Himself which teach that some will be saved and some will be lost. For those who regard neither the Bible as a reliable source nor Jesus as an authoritative teacher, there is no problem. But for a professing Christian it is exceedingly difficult to ignore, 'for the gate is wide and the way is easy, that leads to destruction, and those who enter by it are many',[2] which comes from the Sermon on the Mount.

One way out, for the universalist, is for him to make all the 'pains' of punishment and exclusion to be purgatorial, i.e. a temporary, unpleasant state immediately after death leading to a permanent blessed state later on. The doctrine of purgatory is not a biblical one, though support is found

[1] 1 Timothy 2:3, 4; Philippians 2:10, 11.
[2] Matthew 7:13.

for it in the Apocrypha. But it is outside my immediate concern here. For if there is one thing characteristic of the punishment of the unbeliever as described in Jesus' sayings, it is its finality. Paul's statement that 'They shall suffer the punishment of eternal destruction and exclusion from the presence of the Lord'[3] is entirely in keeping with the pronouncements of Jesus Himself.

A further criticism is to wonder how it is possible for God to bring pressure on the rebellious man so that he changes his mind. And the answer that is given is that He does it by 'irresistible grace'. By His loving power, He so places the rebel and brings such circumstances to bear on him and inflicts him with certain deprivations, that finally the sinful man capitulates in self-surrender. Hick uses the analogy of a novice chess-player pitting himself against a Grand Master. Although every move the novice makes is 'free' the final outcome can be predicted with 'full practical certainty'. The author admits 'This analogy breaks down if pressed beyond a certain point': I would say it breaks down at the crucial point, *viz.* a battle of wills is not just a battle of wits. If it were, then of course God would win every time. But this is *not* the God of the Bible. He is a schemer in the sense that He plans salvation, sends His Son, founds the church and so on. But having set this before us by the proclamation of the gospel, He treats us as responsible agents, not naughty children who have to be outwitted into eating things which we do not like but which are good for us. If He has offered us a choice, it must be possible for some to refuse. This still leaves God, if I may put it so crudely, with a problem as to what to do with such people.

Universalism is all of a piece with an evolutionary view of 'soul-making', which denies a historical Fall and casts doubt on the use of the cross of Jesus. It might be more comfortable than its alternatives, but Jesus did not offer

[3] 2 Thessalonians 1:9.

comfortable thinking any more than He offered comfortable beds. What He did claim to offer was the truth.

Annihilation

In any human institution, there must be a final sanction against persistent offenders. However much a society may try to reform and help its criminals, sooner or later society must use its power to prevent further rebellion. The child is chastised by its parents, the pupil is expelled from the school, the criminal is given a life sentence. The punishment may well have a reformatory effect. But one thing is plain, the rebellious state of affairs cannot be allowed to continue. Authority must use its power.

People who argue with God and ask Him to use His power to 'put the world right' very often forget that His power might first be used on their own rebellion; they forget He is 'like a man of war'.[4] When God sent His Son Jesus into the world, He did not send Him to judge and condemn, but He might have done. The second coming of Jesus is connected with many stories which speak of destruction for those who have refused the offer of rescue (Matthew 25, for instance). One of the most lyrical passages in the Gospels which describes the relationship between Christ and the believer contains harsh talk about people being no better than branches fit to be cut off and thrown on the bonfire.[5] What is, perhaps, the most famous verse in the New Testament, John 3:16, contains a reference to men 'perishing'. It is possible to argue from many places that God's answer to the final rebel is annihilation. God's final sanction is to destroy completely the man who insists on his own will and his own position at the centre, right to the end.

[4] Isaiah 42:13.   [5] John 15:1-11.

The advantage of this alternative is that it is quite consistent with the FWD. Man is acknowledged to be really free and he is overcome in the end only by power. His free will is not tampered with from within, nor is he outwitted by superior intelligence. He maintains his dignity, he chooses and he accepts the result of his choice. From God's side no part of His creation is 'out of control' for all pockets of resistance are eliminated. Indeed, being God, He does not have to 'eliminate' but merely ceases to extend His First Order Approval to this or that individual.

Annihilation however also has its difficulties. The first is an argument: if it is the case that certain human beings are to be wiped out, then the evil that they suffered or perpetrated is quite pointless because it has failed to produce any good. So why did God allow it to start? The second difficulty is that it does not quite do justice to the words of Jesus. He spoke about 'eternal punishment', 'unquenchable fire', 'eternal fire', '. . . outer darkness, there men will weep and gnash their teeth'.[6] All these expressions imply that the awful fate reserved for the rebellious is not instantaneous annihilation. The world 'eternal' is used many times.

Eternal hell

If then we accept the words of Jesus we seem to be driven to a belief in that difficult notion of an eternal hell where God eternally condemns those who have rejected Him and who have no hope of remission. If there is indeed such a condition as hell it might be the biggest part of the problem of evil, for there in God's universe, side by side with all His love and His salvation, there exists a 'pocket of evil' which He can do nothing about and which He can love but will never love Him in return. Furthermore such a doctrine is

[6] Matthew 25:46; Mark 9:43; Matthew 18:8; 25:30.

difficult to reconcile with God's goodness for He must have known, as He created, that such and such a man would finally rebel, and yet He created him knowing that for all eternity He would punish him. And 'punish' is such a wretched term, for God would know that there was no element of reform in such an unending process. So God's creation would be for ever shadowed by this blot. Who could enjoy heaven knowing of its existence? And if the blessed were kept in ignorance, God would know and thus be frustrated. It is hardly surprising that in view of these objections, so many deny the existence or possibility of an eternal hell.

What the Bible does not say

It is so easy to overstate the case against eternal hell that it is worth while removing some conceptions about it that opponents of the doctrine knock down as straw dolls.

First, strictly speaking, although the sentence of condemnation must ultimately be God's, it is man himself who chooses hell. Hell is not like a gaol where prisoners are longing to be free but like a sit-in where the protesters have barricaded themselves in.

Second, God is not a torturer, nor does hell make Him one. The father who sees his son, contrary to advice, ruining his life, is not a torturer. The result of rebellion against God is fixed, not arbitrarily as a torturer selects his thumbscrew or pincers, but because things must be as they are.

Third, hell cannot be 'side by side' with heaven. Heaven is being, hell towards not-being. God is light, hell is outer darkness. The old definition of evil as 'privation of good' has a validity here. Hell is often talked of as 'death' by Jesus. Death does not exist 'side by side' with life. Death is the absence of life.

Fourth, to say that hell is a punishment of retribution

without reform is not necessarily unethical. If you pick up a red-hot poker with your bare hand, you will be burnt. This is 'retribution' but no-one suggests it is immoral. How much more if we break God's laws of the spirit. The law of sin and death may be talked of in legal terms. But sin and death are no more two separate realities than the acorn and the oak. The one is the 'end' of the other.

Fifth and last, the Bible does not say that God made and predestined certain humans to hell. The famous verses in Romans 9:22-24 are cast as a hypothetical speculation. Jesus Himself positively affirms that He has come to seek and save 'the lost'.

What the New Testament does say

First we must turn to the words of Jesus Himself. By using the word *gehenna* (translated in RSV and NEB as 'hell') Jesus evokes for His hearers the *gehenna* or valley of Hinnom situated on the south side of Jerusalem. Hundreds of years before this had been a place of human sacrifice to Molech, but after the abolition of that worship it was used as a rubbish pit. A fire was kept continually burning and maggots bred there. The place became in Jewish thinking a symbol for God's final punishment. The phrase 'where their worm does not die, and the fire is not quenched' occurs at the end of Isaiah's prophecy and also in later Jewish literature. In such passages as Mark 9:43-48, Jesus implores His hearers to do anything rather than to get caught up in this final punishment of hell. God, He says, 'can destroy both soul and body in Gehenna' (Matthew 10:28). The emphasis seems to be on destruction rather than unending torment, though the process of destruction may be frightful.

Two main pictures are used by Jesus to describe the final state of the rebellious. The first is of fire: a 'furnace of fire'

Is referred to in Matthew 13:42, 50 and an 'eternal fire' is mentioned in Matthew 25:41. This latter is said by Jesus to be 'prepared for the devil and all his angels' and in verse 46 is equated with 'eternal punishment'.

The second picture is of 'outer darkness'. This emphasizes the idea of exclusion, for example, from a feast. 'Many will come . . . and sit at table . . . while the sons of the kingdom (*i.e.* rebellious Jews) will be thrown into the outer darkness; there men will weep and gnash their teeth' (Matthew 8: 11, 12). This last phrase occurs six times in the Gospels and heightens the idea of a perpetual punishment for those outside.

Turning to other writers in the New Testament, sixteen times in his letters Paul speaks of the 'wrath' of God as a dreadful reality to be reckoned with. He talks of judgment (with justice) and of death. In 2 Thessalonians 1:9 he speaks of 'the punishment of eternal destruction and exclusion from the presence of the Lord'.

In Peter's second letter (2:17) we read, 'for them the nether gloom of darkness has been reserved' and Jude 13 adds 'for ever'.

John, in the book of Revelation (20:14) records that he had revealed to him 'a lake of fire. This is the second death.'

Hell : a permanent feature?

It would be naïve to write off all this evidence in terms of Jesus' sharing of current misconceptions or to say that all He 'meant' by hell was a local rubbish pit. But it is still not easy to interpret the symbols. I offer what follows as my own interpretation bearing in mind the needs of theodicy. This is a dangerous course since I could be tempted to make the evidence say what I wish to be the case rather than what God has said actually is the case.

First, the symbol of fire. In the Old Testament this is a

symbol of God's presence and in any culture is a symbol of destruction. 'Our God is a consuming fire'[7] is a New Testament reminder that you cannot play with God (argue with God?) and not be harmed. Those who finally rebel against God must still reckon to meet Him but He will be fire to them. The symbol of fire, then, would seem to imply annihilation. But Jesus talked of 'eternal fire'. If by that He means that God is eternal, it does not imply that those who plunge into that lake are also eternal. But this view seems to be negated by the phrase 'eternal punishment'.

The symbol of 'outer darkness' with its wailing inhabitants does seem to imply a permanent state and torment. But I wonder if there is still not room for development within a permanent state. The damned are permanently 'outside' but this does not mean they are just outside, nor that they are for ever clamouring to be let in. What shall we do in heaven? We shall learn more and do more with God and for God; there must be progression, an unfolding as we become more and more human, more and more 'in his image'. What shall men do in hell? Perhaps 'do' is an impossible word, for sin and death and hell are negative ideas. Sin consists of placing oneself at the centre. On this earth we are frequently forced to pay attention to other people or to our environment through our senses, but not in hell. As the sinner goes deeper and deeper into the darkness, cut off from God, increasingly separated from other people, more and more self-centred until self is the only reality, the end of this process is nothing you could recognize as human. This would indeed be Death.

How long would this continue? As soon as we ask the question we know it to be meaningless. We cannot imagine anything outside time, any more than we can imagine anything without the other dimensions of this world. The word 'eternal' is difficult to say the least. But 'eternal life'

[7] Hebrews 12:29.

means something: a life lived with God. Not so 'eternal death'. Death is an end and you cannot have an end with God. Jesus says 'the hour is coming when all who are in the tombs will hear his voice and come forth, those who have done good, to the resurrection of life, and those who have done evil, to the resurrection of judgment'.[8] 'Life' is a process word: but 'judgment' is a crisis word. God's sentence cannot in any sense be parallel to the life he gives to those who trust in Him.

So the dwindling process of the damned man in the darkness may not finally be so very different from the destruction process of the fire. But both pictures prevent us from thinking that to suffer loss after this life is like the annihilation of the hospital anaesthetic. It will be an infinitely painful and agonizing anguish: and it is Jesus Himself who keeps emphasizing this very point.

We are left, then, with grave difficulties for our theodicy. How can God be faced with an eternal, although fading and increasingly unreal, evil in His cosmos? Has He no power? Has God, in fact, suffered a final defeat?

I suspect that this is one of our 'nonsense questions'. In one sense, yes; God is defeated by sin, by the sinner. But who enjoys the fruit of that 'victory'? Not God and certainly not man. The fact that Jesus believed in the eternal fixity of a human choice, once that human has passed beyond this life, encourages me perhaps more than anything else to believe in free will. Hell is a *fantastic* doctrine but it *is* the logical result of giving man free will. The doctrine has been called 'the Bible's breath-taking humanism' that God will take 'no' for an answer from man.[9] God has the power to make man a different being, but He will not use it. Rather than un-make man in heaven, God allows man to un-make himself on his own.

[8] John 5:28, 29.
[9] David L. Edwards, *The Last Things Now* (SCM, 1969), p. 78.

Then why did He make man? Now we really *are* asking impossible questions: we shall never know what might have been.

I should not like to leave this doctrine of hell without saying a word about its purpose. It used to be thought by some that the words of Jesus were given to us so that we could construct a geography of the after-life. Indeed the Bible is still used by some as a kind of pre-history book. But the Bible is not addressed primarily to the intellect, however much we may think about it. It is addressed to the will. Moral evil arises because men choose wrongly; the whole of Jesus' teaching is to make us choose and behave differently. At times He seems to be giving us information, but invariably it has a practical implication. 'I am the door', He says. But it means, 'Enter by me!' If He says He is the bread of life, then He expects us to find nourishment in Him. If He says God is holy, then He expects us to be holy also. If He says it is possible to be eternally judged, then He expects us to believe on Him who can give eternal life.

Some have objected that the doctrine of hell is just a way of frightening men to accept Christianity. But is it immoral to warn men of danger? The question is, not whether hell is frightening, but whether it *is*. If free will is in fact so very dangerous men may be more careful how they exercise it. Others have said that you cannot become a Christian by fear, only by love. This rests on a confusion. A man can be *saved* by fear: he can become like Christ only by love. To suppose that a man lives the Christian life daily in the fear of hell is of course a caricature. But frequently men are so selfishly immersed in life that they need a good-sized jolt to shake them out of it.

No-one need go to hell. Always in the Bible judgment is connected with God's justice. There will be no surprises and God will not make any mistakes. But to suppose that someone who has the Bible readily available in his own language will at the last be somehow excused or cajoled into God's kingdom is to indulge in wishful thinking.

QUESTIONS FOR FURTHER THOUGHT AND DISCUSSION

Consider a man who has blatantly lived a proud, self-centred life, oppressing others, profiting from his injustice and gloating over the downfall of the righteous. Can you will that such a man be allowed to continue after this life still enjoying the last laugh?

'They have Moses and the prophets; let them hear them' (Jesus in Luke 16:29). Is it reasonable to expect a 'second chance' once this life is over? How many people fail to become Christians simply because they cannot be bothered to find out?

8 WHY DOESN'T GOD DO SOMETHING?

If a horse stumbles and breaks a leg, it is usually shot. If a child has earache in the night the parents will give it aspirin. If a boy is being bullied by two others, the schoolmaster will intervene to prevent injustice. Whenever there is suffering, whether physical pain or mental anguish, man-at-his-best will do his best to help. But his powers are so limited. God's power, so they say, is unlimited. So why doesn't He *do* something?

It is not only unbelievers who feel like this. At some time or other every believer who has good reason to believe and to love God feels as though he has been let down 'left, right and centre'. After all, God wouldn't have to do very much to alleviate suffering. Listen again to C. S. Lewis:[1]

> 'What chokes every prayer and every hope is the memory of all the prayers H and I offered and all the false hopes we had. Not hopes raised merely by our own wishful thinking; hopes encouraged, even forced upon us, by false diagnoses, by X-ray photographs, by strange remissions, by one temporary recovery that might have ranked as a miracle. Step by step we were "led up the garden path".'

Well, why doesn't God do something?

The object of this chapter is to show that God *does* do

[1] *A Grief Observed*, p. 26.

something, though He does not inhibit free will, nor is He forever suspending physical laws to make a crazy universe.

God sees and cares

The Israelites were a nation in slavery. Their masters were cruel and their life was bitter. 'And the people of Israel groaned under their bondage, and cried out for help, and their cry under bondage came up to God. And God heard their groaning, and God remembered his covenant . . . And God saw the people of Israel, and God knew their condition.'[2] So begins perhaps the greatest of all the Old Testament stories: the Exodus from Egypt. The assertion is plain, that God sees and cares about suffering in His world. He is not a remote king, far removed from the troubles of His subjects grovelling in the misery of everyday life. There is no 'problem of communication' for Him. He knows exactly what is going on and, what is more, He cares about it.

The Bible goes on in a similar strain. When the prophet Isaiah tells the people God's word they find (to their surprise?) that God knows about the happenings of the market-place as well as about the multiplicity of idols. The irregularities in the law courts, the hidden bribe, the twisted motive, the drunken feasts, the elaborate, luxurious houses, the land-grabbing, the cosmetics, the wardrobes full of the latest fashions; all these are known to God in devastating detail. And He cares. He has heard the cry of the widow and the despair of the frustrated plaintiff.

God suffers

But Hosea reveals an even more amazing side to this knowledge by God of men's affairs. In his living parable Hosea

[2] Exodus 2:23-25.

tells the Israelites (and us) that when His people sin, God suffers. Hosea was married to an unfaithful woman. In spite of his lavishing every care and gift on her she scorned his love and spent wild nights away from home. With complete lack of delicacy Hosea likens God to the deserted husband. The frustration, anger, impatience and deep sorrow that he had experienced, Hosea says, belong to God as well. When men sin, God suffers. When we talk casually of God giving men free will, we might be talking of giving an expensive toy to a child. We think what it will mean to the man, his responsibility, his dignity, his 'divine spark'. But what will it mean for God to give such a gift? Read Hosea's prophecy and find out what sorrow, what suffering, what anguish it is for God to know the despicable detail of man's sin.

In one breath, he decrees their punishment:

'They shall return to the land of Egypt . . .
The sword shall rage against their cities,
    consume the bars of their gates,
    and devour them in their fortresses.'

But then, in the next breath, we have these sublime words:

'How can I give you up, O Ephraim! . . .
How can I make you like Admah! . . .
My heart recoils within me,
    my compassion grows warm and tender.
I will not execute my fierce anger,
    I will not again destroy Ephraim;
for I am God and not man,
    the Holy One in your midst,
    and I will not come to destroy.'[3]

So the Old Testament is the story of God who sees, hears, suffers and acts. God *does* something. He brings His

[3] Hosea 11: 5, 6, 8, 9.

people out of Egypt; He protects them in the wilderness; He leads them to their land; He sends them leaders, priests, prophets, kings; He judges them in exile and brings them back home. He makes promises and fulfils them. He does not always act as expected, but He hears the cry of the oppressed and is the deliverer of those who suffer.

Jesus as a clearer revelation

But it is in the New Testament that God is revealed more completely. 'He who has seen me has seen the Father'[4] said Jesus. What do we see of Jesus when He meets evil, whether in moral man or in the disease-death environment?

The first and most obvious comment is that Jesus was most positively and actively opposed to evil. Life, which is often grey to us, was black and white to Him. If a lie was told by a friend, He addresses that friend as 'Satan'. If He finds that religious leaders are proud and hypocritical He calls them 'children of hell'. If He finds a morally upright young man who has still not made the vital decision to put God first, He tells him 'You lack one thing'. When a man flatteringly asks for advice about some rules of estate management, He says bluntly, 'Take heed, and beware of all covetousness'. Nowhere is there any compromise.[5]

In a similar way He fights disease. All who are diseased and brought to Him are healed.[6] God is doing something! There is a remarkable amount of space in the Gospels devoted to 'miracles' of healing: remove all such incidents and the narratives are in tatters. It is the same when He meets men possessed with 'unclean spirits'. Whether or not you call these psychological disorders, Jesus *did* something to relieve human suffering. He even grappled with death

[4] John 14:9.
[5] Matthew 16:23; 23:15; Mark 10:21; Luke 12:15.
[6] Matthew 8:16.

itself, as in the case of Lazarus and the widow's son. And on more than one occasion when a natural 'catastrophe' threatened to overwhelm His disciples He stilled the storm.

When Jesus came, the kingdom of God indeed had already come close. God is opposed to the evil in His creation: evil is His implacable enemy. His answer to John the Baptist in prison is that the enemy's power is beginning to crack. 'Go and tell John what you have seen and heard: the blind receive their sight, the lame walk, lepers are cleansed, and the deaf hear, the dead are raised up, the poor have good news preached to them.'[7] No wonder the people were excited: God has visited and redeemed His people!

But Jesus not only fought the evil that threatens man: He identified Himself with man in his position in a fallen world.

First there is the bare and staggering fact of the incarnation itself. 'Tears and smiles like us He knew.' Born into a humble family and a subject nation He knew what it was to be taunted for lack of education or to be commandeered for Roman service. He saw people hungry, and grieved over them. He spoke with haughty men and loved them still. He chose a man to be His friend who later betrayed Him. He threw Himself open to the jealous attack of those who should have been His best disciples. He had to listen to the bickering of His friends when His mind was on more important matters. The picture of Jesus in the Gospels is one of a man completely immersed in human life, but not a sinner. All the frustrations, worries, anxieties and vulnerabilities of the human position were His. He worked with His hands, He travelled on His feet. He slept, He wept, He walked, He talked. Sympathy literally means 'suffering with': everything that could be shared by the

[7] Luke 7:22-23.

sinless Son of God with sinful man was shared and experienced. I do not suppose for a moment that the incarnation increased God's knowledge of man, but it does increase man's knowledge of God. For there He is, one of us!

Again the note of Hosea is struck in Jesus' grieving over the city of Jerusalem:

> 'How often would I have gathered your children together as a hen gathers her brood under her wings, and you would not!'[8]

and again

> 'When he drew near and saw the city he wept over it, saying, "Would that even today you knew the things that make for peace!".'[9]

If you feel like saying 'Why doesn't God do something? Doesn't He care?' then look at Jesus in the Gospels. He spent His whole life caring. And what He cared about more than anything else was the sinful ways of man. When people say 'Doesn't God care?' they are usually talking about what they are suffering, either from someone else's sin or from the disease-death environment: they are not usually talking about the effect that their injustice or sin is having on someone else. We see Jesus weeping with the mourners, but we also see Him weeping over rebellious man and his false choices.

Even now we have not reached the heart of the matter. If Jesus' suffering had stopped with grieving over man's rebellion there would be no gospel and no hope. But Jesus also identified Himself with the sin of man. As a result He died on a Roman gallows. The story is so well known that it has inevitably lost some of its startling unexpected-

[8] Luke 13:34.   [9] Luke 19:41.

ness. When men say that Jesus was a great teacher or a good example (meaning *merely* a teacher or *merely* an example) they are just watering the story down to what one might expect to be the truth. But the actual story has the sort of surprise that the real and living God might well spring. You might possibly have guessed that God would do a kind of King Henry V in the incarnation and wander among His subjects in disguise. But that He should then propose to take *on Himself* the total effect of all the evil of mankind is quite staggering. You would think that if God suddenly confronted man in the midst of the years, He would fairly lay all the evil and its effects firmly where they belonged, on the backs of men. But John says, 'For God sent the Son into the world, not to condemn the world, but that the world might be saved through him.'[10] Paul says that 'Christ Jesus came into the world to save sinners'. "[11]

As the song we quoted in chapter 5 goes on:

> 'It's God they ought to crucify
> Instead of you and me
> I said to the carpenter
> A-hanging on the tree.'

What the crucified criminal didn't know was the whole point: that he was talking to God.

Now if the Christian claim is true then what it means is this: that God created man free; that free men have chosen wrongly and bespattered life with moral evil; that God determined to deal with this moral evil; that God sent His Son to grapple personally with this evil; that the price for this struggle was an agonizing death; that God foresaw this agony in that the Scripture says that Jesus was 'delivered up according to the definite plan and foreknowledge of God'.[12]

[10] John 3:17.   [11] 1 Timothy 1:15.   [12] Acts 2:23.

The implications of this teaching for theodicy are tremendous. In the first place when men say 'Why doesn't God do something about evil in the world?', the plain straight answer is 'He has. He sent His only Son to die in order to deal with it.' God has done everything possible, short of un-making man and depriving him of his free will.

In the early pages of the Bible there is recorded a story of an earlier theophany. Confronted with the gravest moral evil God sent a flood of destruction to eliminate those evil beings on the earth. He started again with Noah. Noah's successors also sinned and the New Testament describes God's dealing with evil at a more fundamental level. It is natural to ask *how* it is that Christ's death saves us from evil. But that is another subject. It is enough for our purposes to state that according to the original Christian documents, and hence Christian belief, Christ *did* bear away sin and that Christians have always testified to His power to forgive and to give new moral power. So to charge God with failing to act is to be absurd. God has acted in a way one would not have thought possible: in Christ He humbled Himself and submitted to death.

In the second place, Jesus Himself experienced the 'problem of evil'. In one place, He said, 'I saw Satan fall like lightning from heaven' as He saw the evil power beginning to break; but on the cross He cried 'My God, my God, why hast thou forsaken me?' When we consider Jesus' great knowledge of God and His purposes, His own innocence plus His certainty of the resurrection, we glimpse what man must always feel as he is overwhelmed by the evil in the world. This evil is not imaginary. And God seems far off, just when He is needed. There is no greater proof that Jesus was truly man than in this cry of dereliction.

But third, we must not forget that Jesus was divine as

well. The history of the cross is two-sided: Jesus died; but also God gave. We have been allowed to witness some of the agony on earth: what of the suffering in heaven? The most fundamental concept we have of God is of love. But in that love there is contained deep suffering. People who attack theism often depict God as deliberately choosing between a set of possibilities and then in some inexplicable way choosing a world full of sin and suffering and rapine. But the Christian gospel says that He chose the one that included the suffering and death of His Son; that when He created the suffering was already there. When a tree is felled, we see the rings as a slice of time. The crucifixion is like that. But the rings run right up the trunk: they are not rings but cylinders. The fullness of the rings is hidden to the eye, but the full growth and reality of the tree is in those hidden things. So with God's love-in-suffering. At certain moments in time, by the voice of a prophet, supremely by the death of Christ, we glimpse this compassionate love. But the reality is far greater, the truly stupendous cost that God Himself undertook when He decided to create 'in his own image'.

What do you suggest?

It might be helpful to contrast what God has done with what He might do to alleviate a particular evil. Let us suppose that a friend has been badly injured in a car smash, what could God do or have done?

1 He could suspend physical laws at the moment of impact so that inertia could not do its destructive work.

2 He could over-rule the judgment or the will of the driver of the offending car just before the collision.

3 He could have hindered the research that produced motor-cars in the first place.

4 He could instantaneously heal those who were injured.

Sooner or later these alternatives resolve themselves into two major ones:

1 God could un-make man by withdrawing free will and direct the course of all things personally.

2 God could interfere in a series of special providences to negate the evil effects of bad choices.

But even the second of these is the first in disguise, because if all my evil choices issue in nil effect then I might as well not have chosen; certainly there is no motive to choose right – or drive carefully. If I know that whatever I do God will over-rule all the evil I may do, why should I worry? The whole notion of purpose is removed and life would be very different. Would it be better? I doubt it, but then this is another nonsense question like saying, 'Would I like to be Jones?' If 'I' were Jones, I would be no longer 'I'.

I was hungry

There is a very suggestive phrase that comes in one of Jesus' parables of the last judgment (Matthew 25:31-46). When the king confronts the 'goats', those who have consistently led self-centred lives, He accuses them of failing to succour and minister to Him when He was hungry, thirsty, naked, sick, a stranger or in prison. The defendants, understandably indignant, claim that they have never seen the king in such circumstances. And He replies, 'Truly, I say to you, as you did it not to one of the least of these, you did it not to me.'

Now this of course may be just a manner of speaking, a form of words. But that phrase 'I was hungry' could mean a lot more now that we see God revealed through the cross of

Christ. It could mean what it says: that there is no kind of suffering where God is not there in person. That if we leave people starving we are actually increasing God's agony: if we feed them God never forgets that we have also 'helped' Him. If a sparrow cannot fall to the ground without His knowledge then God must be there, 'feeling' as well as 'knowing'.

Who will argue with such a God as this? Already we feel ready to drop our pens or our ploughs and to get out into all the evil in the world and start doing something. The problem of evil is certainly not theoretical for God: it is a matter for action.

QUESTIONS FOR FURTHER THOUGHT AND DISCUSSION

Can you analyse why Jesus is so attractive in the Gospels when He is such a resounding failure?

If Jesus was a product of His day and of contemporary thinking, how do you account for the fact that He so bitterly criticized the 'church' establishment of His time?

9 WHY DON'T YOU DO SOMETHING?

Already we have felt a stirring to action. We noticed in chapter 2 that there are two problems raised by the existence of evil, one theoretical and one practical. The practical problem is that we condemn evil in others but still take part in the same things ourselves. The theoretical problem is only a problem if you believe in the God who is the Father of Jesus Christ. But because there is a Father of the *crucified* Christ we see a glimmer of light. There is more than a glimmer if you want to tackle the practical problem.

The practical problem is everybody's problem. Not everyone has a taste for theoretical argument but everyone must face life as it comes – and it usually comes in large lumps. What we most readily complain about and groan under is the 'blow' that comes from outside, either from disease or from someone's malice or carelessness. But it is no use praying 'Thy kingdom come', thinking of all the evils that are in the world, unless you are prepared to pray 'Thy kingdom come' for the only area where you have any real control: in your own life and decisions. We all want help with the struggles of life, but first we *need* help with the struggle over inward sin. Jesus told an absurd story about a man with a plank of wood in his eye trying to extract a speck of dust from his brother's eye. If you really dislike 'evil' so much then start with yourself.

Yourself first

The greatest evil in your own area is your own personal rebellion against God. It is no good beginning with your relationships with other people: those must wait. You must begin with *the* relationship. If you have no pastor to whom you can easily turn you can do no better than read the first five chapters of Paul's letter to the Romans. Read it in a modern translation such as the New English Bible until you get the feel of it. You may want to read more, but at this stage don't go past chapter 8. You will find there set out the chief components of the Christian good news. Man is sinful (who can get past the list in chapter 1?); God is merciful (Christ has died); Christ is no longer dead but offers His Spirit to live within man; vital union is the relationship between Christ and the believer; He takes our sin and death, we take His life and victory; once the decision of repentance and faith is taken, the believer is secure; nothing can touch him, nothing can overcome him; the Christian is safe in the love of God.

What follows then is the Christo-centric life instead of the egocentric. This calls for a real decision – the opposite decision from the one Adam made. Do not doubt that you can make it, but it *is* a big decision. From now on it will be 'Christ first' in every part of life. This is what the classic words of repentance and faith mean. Repentance means 'not I'; faith means 'but Christ'. You turn from self to Christ – this is not two things but one. It is a deliberate re-centring of your life.

You do not become perfect immediately but you are 'adopted' into God's family immediately and you are 'joined to Christ' immediately. You have a secure bond with Him who has overcome sin and death and suffering and all the rest. Only on this basis can you now face the evil world.

Your relationships

Now you are ready to tackle some of the evil in the world. 'So far as it depends upon you, live peaceably with all', said Paul to the Romans (12:18). The second evil (B) we defined as 'man's inhumanity to man'[1] and you have had your share in that. You now have a different basis on which to deal with other people. One very important difference is that now you have humbled yourself before God it is so much easier to be humble before other people. The Christian is the man who has learnt to say 'I'm sorry'. And how many quarrels would be quickly resolved with just that simple admission?

The Christian is the man who is forgiven: so he finds it much easier to forgive. Jesus' story of the Two Servants in Matthew 18 brilliantly illustrates this. If you have been let off a debt of millions of pounds, will you sue your brother for a fiver? So the Christian's indebtedness and gratitude to God will influence him in all the petty spites he has to bear.

The Christian is the man who has been given much: so he finds it easier to give. He doesn't find it a hardship to provide for some of the needs of others and God never lets him go in want because he has given. By gifts of money, by voluntary service, economies can be developed, people can be fed, children protected, disasters mitigated.

The man who has become a Christian need no longer feel frustrated in the place where he works. God has put him there for a purpose and if it is right to move He will make it plain. The Christian will not opt out of his work because it has become a rat-race, but it will cease to be a rat-race for him, and so the race itself is lessened.

The Christian sees his fellow in a new light, as one for whom Christ died. So he tells him the gospel and maybe his

[1] See pp. 29f., 36-39.

friend also turns to Christ. No wonder there is joy in the presence of God as the level of evil perceptibly falls. Wherever there is a Christian working as 'salt' and 'light', God's load is lightened and many will bless the day they met him.

And then there is the area of political and economic decisions which improve or waste the environment or which redistribute wealth and comfort more or less equitably. The man in a position of great responsibility who has become a Christian now has the Spirit of truth to guide him into all truth. God wants to guide him and use him as a prophet for the benefit of all. All Christians, however, have some voice in political decisions and we must speak and vote as men in touch with God. Above all we can pray for our leaders that mistakes may not be repeated and that wise policies may be formulated.

There is a remarkable story in the book *Miracle on the River Kwai* about a man who had to go to a Japanese prisoner-of-war camp to find out what life was all about. There amidst all the disease, filth, brutality, malnutrition and exhaustion he found men who lived by serving others. He discovered that these things were 'anti-life': selfishness, hatred, envy, jealousy, greed, self-indulgence, laziness, pride. But the 'essence of life' was: love, heroism, self-sacrifice, sympathy, mercy, integrity, creative faith. 'They turned mere existence into living in its truest sense.'[2] This is the very stuff of life. God is love, God gave. God is also life. So living is loving and giving. But you will never persuade your unbeliever of this. Know God in your life first and you will discover His secrets.

Death

At the end of Romans 8 there is a list of things which cannot separate the Christian from the love of God. The

[2] E. Gordon, *Miracle on the River Kwai* (Fontana, 1965), p. 121.

list covers virtually everything as it names 'things present' and 'things to come'.

Let us take death first. The Christian's own death hardly worries him at all, for what the world calls 'death' he calls 'being with Christ, which is far better'. As time goes on we increasingly discover how little this life, *in itself*, has to offer, and we begin to long for our 'real home'. There is no security or lasting satisfaction in this world; we get sickened of the battle with evil, we despair of making one convert. Let's join the family party! In Hebrews, men are described as 'through fear of death subject to lifelong bondage'.[3] Not the Christian: for him 'death' brings the focus of his ambition.

The death of others will hit him harder. The nagging sense of loss, especially if the bond was a close one, can wear down a strong man. But there is ample strength in the Scriptures once the first frenzy of grief has died down. Is not God the God of the living?

'We would not have you ignorant, brethren, concerning those who are asleep, that you may not grieve as others do who have no hope. For since we believe that Jesus died and rose again, even so, through Jesus, God will bring with him those who have fallen asleep.'[4]

Disease and disaster

Those blows which come suddenly and without warning for the Christian are not 'blows of fate'. For nothing comes to him but it brings God to him as well. God is closer than disease or disaster and it is the Christian's conviction that these things cannot separate him from the love of God in Christ.

Disease is difficult. Jesus unequivocally declared war on disease and always conquered it. His disciples were given a

[3] Hebrews 2:15.   [4] 1 Thessalonians 4:13, 14.

similar power to heal and even to raise the dead. Yet in these days we are content to leave the healing to doctors and the drugs. Some groups of Christians feel very strongly that the church's ministry of healing should be revived and indeed some do with a measure of 'success', if that is the right word. 'The prayer of faith will save the sick' says the Scripture,[5] but this is a general rule rather than an unbreakable one, unless 'save' means more than 'heal'. Paul himself speaks of a 'thorn in the flesh' which three times he asked to be removed and it was not. He had to be content with 'My grace is sufficient for you, for my power is made perfect in weakness'.[6]

There is no doubt that even the Christian is easily tempted to be self-sufficient and self-reliant as he was in the days of his darkness. Sometimes God allows a blow to come which prevents pride creeping in. It is a great mistake to think that a certain spiritual battle has been won once and for all. The Christian often finds himself fighting over familiar ground and he has to learn his lesson all over again.

One thing is certain: the Christian is not exempt from disease and disaster. One is in a road smash, another loses his child on a swing, another has cancer. Perhaps if Christians were exempt it would first make them high-minded and secondly provide too much 'compulsion' for others to be converted. Just as Jesus came, so the Christian must still be identified with the world and is bound up with it until the last day. One possible interpretation of Jesus' ministry of healing is that as He brought the last things with Him, so the disappearance of disease is one of them. After all death itself will vanish one day but this did not mean that Jesus raised all those who died near Him. Those who have been healed, even raised to life, are a token, a foretaste, of what is to come.

[5] James 5:15.   [6] 2 Corinthians 12:9.

'Pain' in the simple sense of being the warning system of the body that something is malfunctioning can hardly be regarded as evil. If I have a stomach-ache, I take either a pill or a pastry according to the nature of the ache. No, by pain I mean the kind that leads to suffering; the extended pain which brings mental anguish that dreads to have more. Very often pain seems to be excessive in that one could imagine it might have been less just to let one know there is something wrong.

C. S. Lewis has an interesting theory about pain and suffering as an aid to people becoming Christians. 'God whispers to us in our pleasures, speaks in our conscience but shouts in our pains: it is His megaphone to rouse a deaf world.'[7] I know a pastor who would say when visiting in hospital, 'Men are like pigs; they only look up when they are on their backs.' I am not saying that is why God gives us suffering, but this is certainly the use He makes of the suffering that exists in the world.

In 2 Corinthians 6 Paul gives a list of the things that he has suffered since he became a Christian: afflictions, hardships, calamities, beatings, imprisonments, tumults, labours, watching, hunger. The word for affliction literally means 'pressure': a word used elsewhere of child-birth. The simile is apt, for the pains we bear are not an end in themselves but a prelude to something greater. Paul talks about 'this slight momentary affliction preparing for us an eternal weight of glory beyond all comparison'. This may not be much help to someone lying on a bed not knowing whether to laugh or cry, but it is a theme which recurs.

[7] *The Problem of Pain* (Blesn, 1940), p. 81.

Suffering as a Christian

By the time Peter wrote his first letter it is clear that the church was going through a tough time. A new kind of suffering is here. Not only are Christians not exempt from the 'natural' pain and suffering of this world, they qualify for an extra kind of suffering just because they *are* Christians. Their faith is being tested by 'fire' quite possibly in a literal sense. In this epistle Peter gave some straight advice:

1 Take suffering without resentment

Left to ourselves we fret and we fume and we fear. We cry 'It's not fair'. But we should take an example from Jesus. 'He committed no sin ... When he was reviled, he did not revile in return' (2:22 f.). Nothing warps and twists the human character like resentment. It is essentially self-centred, as though in some way we had a *right* to certain things. The Christian has no rights except to be loved by God, and that only because He has promised it.

2 Take suffering by trusting God

To have no resentment is negative. To have faith is positive. How did Jesus survive His ordeal without lashing out at His torturers? 'When he suffered, he did not threaten; but he trusted to him who judges justly' (2:23).

It is a truism to say that the Christian life is a life of faith: but that is what it is. Faith means you cannot *see* where you are going or the purpose of what you are doing (or what is being done to you!). You *believe*. You believe that behind all and in control there is a God who 'judges justly'; a God who will not make any mistakes. He weighs all things and soon or late all wrong things will be put right.

3 Take suffering for a little while

We have already noticed this in Paul's letters. Twice in Peter's first letter the phrase 'a little while' occurs. The present unhappy state of affairs is transitory: do not despair. In both places the 'little while' of suffering is compared with the full glory of what awaits the Christian. A man may spend three days climbing Mt Kilimanjaro in Tanzania: more than 30 miles to walk, 15,000 ft to climb. The muscles ache, the lungs strain, the sweat falls. Why bother? Because there's a good view from the top. The guides weave a garland of everlasting flowers for those who make it: a wreath that fades. Is it worth it? Of course! It's not only in mountain walking that men endure hardship in order to achieve success: is it incredible that the greatest prize of all should be accompanied by some suffering? For a little while? It need not be thought that the pains we bear *earn* us a place in heaven. Only Christ's pains can do that for us. But our pains are not pointless, nor endless.

4 Take suffering without surprise

The deepest truth for the Christian about pain and suffering is that he is called to do it. 'If when you do right and suffer for it you take it patiently, you have God's approval. For to this you have been *called*, because Christ also suffered for you, leaving you an example, that you should follow in his steps' (2:20, 21).

To the non-Christian this is nonsense: but then so is the cross of Christ. The notion of a God who suffers from the moment He lays the foundation-stone of the universe is quite unintelligible to one who has never seen love. But to the Christian who has met God through the cross of Christ, love-in-suffering is now his vocation. We all agree that we should love one another: few do so as men of the cross.

We all agree we should become like Christ, but who wants to end on a gibbet? With devastating logic Jesus says, 'Do you want to come after me? Yes? Do you know where I am going? To a cross! Do you still want to come? Then take up your cross, leave self behind and come with me!' (see Luke 9:23).

In practice, when suffering comes, the Christian (if he is anything like me) says 'Why me? Why should this happen? Am I not a child of God?' He regards suffering as an interruption, an unwelcome interlude. When it is over he can get on once more with living a 'fruitful' Christian life. Not so; suffering *is* the Christian life. 'Since therefore Christ suffered in the flesh, arm yourselves with the same thought ...' (1 Peter 4:1). And then in 4:12, 13 Peter says, 'Beloved, do not be surprised at the fiery ordeal which comes upon you to prove you, as though something strange were happening to you. But rejoice in so far as you share Christ's sufferings . . .'.

The cross of Christ is history's supreme example of innocent suffering: but it is matched by the resurrection which is the supreme exhibition of God's vindication of the righteous. So Peter continues, '. . . that you may also rejoice and be glad when his glory is revealed' (4:13).

Arguments and grace

If you should be a Christian and the victim of some great evil, whether it be a phantom in your own mind or a pain-wracked body, then arguments will not help you. Knowledge is not the weal for every woe, as Plato thought. What you need is the grace of God. Arguments may help you not to sin against God, but they did not help Job very much. The quotation of Scripture may help you, as it did when Jesus faced Satan in the wilderness, but sometimes the words of the Bible seem to be written for better men than us. So you need help. Direct help from the Spirit of God. There is only one condition for receiving help and that is humility. 'God gives grace to the humble' says Peter and all the rest. To come to the end of your resources is a happy state, for then you grow desperate. And desperate men find God.

When the pressure is removed, how quickly our human pride starts rebuilding the pitiful façades of self-sufficiency. We do not learn our lessons easily. So here is another reason why God does not immediately remove Christians from this 'naughty world'. We thought when we first came to a point of decision (and how important that is!) that we had placed Christ at the centre. Well, we may have done in principle, but self keeps sneaking in, sidling up the corridors of power and sitting in the seat of authority once more, 'seeing what it feels like'. And then the mailed fist of evil, pain and suffering comes hammering at the door and we remember once more that we have edged out the only Master who has real power to help.

QUESTION FOR FURTHER THOUGHT AND DISCUSSION

If there is no God, how do you account for the fact that people who have experienced great suffering frequently become 'nicer' people?

10 THE BEGINNING OF THE END

'I am the first and the last.' These words could only have been spoken by one person. A man may have the good fortune to be the first in a particular scientific field: he does not have the last word on the subject as well. These words could only be spoken by the Creator. If He made all that there is, then only He could know the purpose of that making.

We have already noticed that there are certain activities of man which mark him off from the rest of the world: ability to choose with understanding; ability to love; ability to criticize himself; ability to say 'what ought to be' even though the evidence provided by his senses is only 'what is'. Here is another unique ability of man: to be able to work and strive towards an 'end'. Man is a teleological being. It is true that at the level of practical reasoning chimpanzees have been seen to arrange boxes in a pile so that they might reach a bunch of bananas suspended from a ceiling. Egyptian vultures, they say, use stones to break open ostriches' eggs. But neither of those activities is to be compared with the level of man's aims, the complexity with which he invests the word 'purpose'. In order to achieve success in an examination or a qualification a man will subordinate his natural desires and interests for months, even years. Analysed on the basis of 'what is' his behaviour can seem almost irrational. The only real meaning to be found in his activity is in the 'end' of his labours.

His friends may ask 'Is it worth it?' We do not find the man unreasonable if he says 'Wait and see'. We certainly do not judge him in terms of his present restrictions but are content to judge the man's actions by the whole, that is by the End as well as the Beginning. When the Creator says 'I am the first and last', He is saying 'Wait and see'. Is this unreasonable? Certainly not! A child may find it unreasonable that his father spends too much time writing his thesis for a PhD, but we do not judge the thesis on the child's opinion. We say to the child, 'One day when your understanding has developed (provided you follow the right kind of studies) you will be able to see why your father didn't play as much football with you as you would have liked.'

God is the first

Opponents of Christianity invoke the doctrine of the Creator as a main plank in their argument that He is thus *responsible* for all that exists. What they often fail to notice is that the idea of Creator contains the idea of a *purposeful* Maker and that it might be worth trying to find out what that purpose is before telling Him what a mess He has made of it.

One of the most useful 'tool' questions a biologist, biochemist or zoologist can ask is 'What's it for?' Faced with a stray iron atom in a vast haemoglobin molecule, the scientist says 'What's it for?' He does not, of course, imply therefore that 'nature' or 'God' plans it to be there, because such concepts are outside the logical framework of his investigation. But scientists still go on asking the question. In contrast to the lively optimism of early science, today the answer 'We don't know' is being given more and more to the question 'What's it for?' The further actual frontiers of knowledge are pushed back the further conceivable horizons recede. It is an age of increasing scientific agnosticism; the cleverest men say 'Wait and see'.

We do not find the same judiciously suspended judgment in pronouncements on the dealings of God with man. 'Look what God has done: it's scandalous!' This may, of course, be spoken in blasphemy; that is, the speaker has made a decision to accept that there is something 'out there' and that he has no use for it, and if he had the chance he would give it a piece of his mind. But it may be, and more often is, spoken in sheer ignorance. We keep admitting that we are limited and finite but do not allow this to stop us making ultimate adverse judgments about our Creator. In the laboratory the scientist may say 'Look what (God) has done! It's most mysterious and rather exciting.' But let that same man read the Bible, or talk to a Christian, and he will say 'Look what God has done! It's monstrous!'

God is the last

At this point in time we may be in a position to make derogatory remarks about the way God has 'arranged' things. But at the End we shall have to *meet* him. In the book of Job all the familiar arguments are trotted out: calamity is judgment for sin; if you are suffering you must be a secret sinner; it is inconceivable that a righteous God rules the world; the answer to suffering is to repent. But the book concludes not with an argument, but an event. Job is confronted with the End who is also the Beginning. God reveals Himself in a whirlwind and above all in His words. And the first thing He says is 'Who is this that darkens counsel by words without knowledge?' There then follows from the mouth of God an incomplete catalogue of His work as Creator and the wonder of it. The final sentence of this speech is: 'Shall a fault-finder contend with the Almighty? He who argues with God, let him answer it.'

Centuries later men are in a far better position to know the wonder of creation. But while some investigators find that their work stimulates their desire to worship there are many, 'liberated' by their new attitude to the world, who become little better than 'fault-finders'.

God is the End. For Him this is the same as the Beginning. But for us the End is different from the Beginning in one important aspect: we shall be there. 'Prepare to meet your God' is not an empty threat: it is a sober warning.

It might be thought that in Job's case the matter is settled not by argument but by *power*. That in effect God is making the evils to be good just by saying so. God is cheating like the heavy-handed headmaster who is asked why junior boys may not cross the grass and replies 'Because it is the rule'. When the basis of the rule is asked he replies 'Because I say so'. Further questioning will only result in punishment. The headmaster's views are imposed by force.

But believers in heaven will not be in the position of crushed schoolboys sadly shaking their heads saying 'I still can't understand it. He said it was the best world He could make, but . . . look out, here He comes!' We shall be convinced, if that is not too weak a word, by the whole. There will be a wealth of extra data to assimilate and enjoy. I imagine this will take some 'time'. No doubt we shall be satisfied on the *personal* level once the 'face to face' experience has been granted. But on the *intellectual* level it is hard to grasp the extent of what will be available. Even in our present state of knowledge, here on earth, a man cannot possibly master in one life-time all there is to know about, say, chemistry.

Included in this wealth of material will be the data needed to solve the problem of evil. We shall doubtless be able to see and grasp more clearly the necessity of creating beings who have scope to rebel. We shall understand this 'antinomy' (as we call it now) of man's responsibility and God's sovereignty. First Order and Second Order support or approval will no longer puzzle us. Even choice itself will take on an entirely new significance when we can know the results of any particular action. We shall also see with our own eyes the 'eternal weight of glory beyond all comparison' of which Paul speaks. It is not to be compared with 'the slight momentary affliction' under which we exist at the moment. The sceptic may reply sarcastically, 'This glory will have to be pretty colossal to compensate for the vast sum of misery at present in the world.' To which of course the believer can reply (without absurdity), 'Yes it will, and I'm greatly looking forward to tasting it.'

The main point is, we shall be satisfied. We shall never be able to think *all* God's thoughts after Him, for you would have to *be* God in order to do that. But from our viewpoint as creatures (and creatures in God's image at that) we shall see as much of the eternal dance as we are able and in that viewing will find a delight and an appreciation of which our present theatre-going is a parody. Nor shall we be mere spectators, for the dance will not be complete without us; and this I take to be one more side of the truth that Christians are members of the body of Christ.

Before I come back to earth, I would like to make one more speculation. I wonder if the main piece of extra evidence relevant to the problem of evil will be this. We have already seen that Christ on His cross took the sin and suffering of the world on His own shoulder; that this suffering is shared by God the Father in the very act of separation from His Son; that God 'absorbed' the whole sting of sin and dealt with it in such a way that if a man wishes he can be completely set free from it. We have seen that it is possible to think of God suffering as the victim,

Is it possible to think of God as immanently suffering in the sinner himself?

We are accustomed to over-simplify the relation between the Creator and His creature. Sometimes we speak of it like father and son, two independent persons on, more or less, equal footing. At other times we speak of Him inside us 'deep down', like some sort of nuclear force-field. But the reality is more complex than this. Suppose I sin – let us say, I tell a lie. God continues to support and hold my body together – this is what we have called 'First Order Approval' (He is immanent). But God is outraged that once more a free subject of His is in rebellion and He looks on me in judgment (He is transcendent). But perhaps there is a third way of looking at the situation. Already by breaking the divine order *I* am beginning to suffer. But is not God suffering too? My 'image of God' has been defiled, I am opposing my true nature, setting up tension inside. There is also tension outside between me and the person who believes the lie. God's gift of the word (given to no other animal) has been devalued. Is God not immanent in my spirit as well as my body? If I suffer, does He not suffer?

I take this argument to mean that God has 'under-written' and carried right into Himself the incalculable suffering of the whole universe. The spectacle of Him merely sitting above the earth, 'arranging' things, watching with detached interest the suffering of His creatures, measuring that suffering with delicate cosmic galvano-meters and comparing it with equally sensitive readings on the good side, and finally deciding that 'on balance, old chap' He thinks it worth while to create, this is indeed revolting. But I do not find this picture of God in the Bible. Jesus describes a man who, before building a tower, sits down and works out if he can afford it. Having decided to pay the price, he puts the work in hand. What sort of calculations did God make before creating? One thing seems to me self-evident: that every particle of suffering in the whole belongs to Him as subject. He underwrote the whole cost Himself. Every time a rabbit is pursued, or a widow cries, or a man acts like a beast, God is there bearing it all. He reckons it's 'worth it' and so do those who understand Him best. During our arguments we have repeatedly said that God is 'responsible' for all the suffering because He is Creator. As Redeemer He has carried that responsibility.

Back to earth

But can we live *now* with the problem of evil? Let us summarize some of the arguments we have made in thinking about the problem. How far have we succeeded?

1 We admit that evils in the world count logically as arguments against the existence of a loving God.

2 We have seen that love nearly always contains pain as indicated by parent-child, husband-wife relationships.

3 We have suggested that while man in a state of sin has God's First Order Approval (that is He wills his continued existence) he has *not* God's Second Order Approval as a moral agent. Man in a state of sin is 'responsible' for himself. Anything less than this makes him a puppet.

4 God deliberately limited His own power in creating such free beings; the logical ground for this being that 'love' cannot exist except against a background of choice and therefore the possibility of failure.

5 This freedom has resulted in the evils we have designated A and B (see chapter 2). You cannot say God is 'responsible' for these, as *a moral agent*, any more than a husband is 'responsible' for his wife's infidelity.

6 My estimate is that evils A and B cause 19/20ths of the human race's misery. If I say that 19/20ths of our

problem is thus 'solved' I do not mean logically, but persuasively (logically the difficulty is intact).

7 The remaining 1/20th is still greatly aggravated by man's attitudes of A and B. The effects of the C and D evils are vastly mitigated by doing what the Christian God tells us to do.

8 The cross of Jesus reveals a *suffering* God and we have shown that it is possible for God to be immanent in the agonizing whole. He is *not* the detached spectator of the original argument.

9 The problem and its argument can only be broken by a final view of the necessity and 'glory' of what God has done throughout creation and redemption. But this cannot be presented with facts until the Last Day. We can only *believe* that the whole is 'worth it'. Flew says this must be 'massive belief'. All right, but the problem of evil is *not* a contradiction in the heart of Christian theology.

This leads to one final question. If it requires 'massive' belief to accept God in creation it seems unlikely that arguments about the problem of evil will induce men to believe. If our arguments have achieved anything, then they have cleared the ground for the enquirer. He need not fear that he must commit intellectual suicide should he decide on other grounds to believe in Christ. But are there 'other grounds'? I will indicate briefly one line of thought.

The resurrection of Jesus

The words 'I am the first and the last' are found in the mouth of Jesus in Revelation 1:17. This implies, as we have seen, that He is Creator. But these words are followed by '. . . and the living one; I died, and behold I am alive for evermore'. Jesus links the beginning and the end with His resurrection. Why is the event so important?

In the first place the resurrection took place in history and is subject to the criteria of true history like any other event.[1] Secondly, the resurrection is the ground of the church. Remove the resurrection and the Acts of the Apostles falls to pieces. To believe in this historic event is implicitly to accept the claims of Jesus to be Saviour and to be Lord of all. He is alive now. It is possible to draw on His life now as an ontological reality and not as a convenient psychological fiction. Millions of otherwise sane and responsible citizens find little difficulty in rejoicing in this experience of the living Christ.

But there is another consideration: we noticed that the problem of innocent suffering discussed in Job concluded not with a Humpty-Dumpty-nice-knock-down-argument-for-you, but with an event. In the New Testament the theoretical problem of innocent suffering is not discussed at all (unless you count John 9:1-3). Instead, in the gospel, there is portrayed the supreme example in history of innocent suffering – the death of Jesus of Nazareth. There is no real parallel to it. You can argue indefinitely about who was responsible: the Jews, the Romans, Pilate, Iscariot, the disciples (even God!)? But no-one seriously suggests that Jesus was responsible. He died an innocent.

So the death of Christ must provoke once more the age-old cry 'Why doesn't God *do* something?' Well, He did. He raised Jesus from the dead and 'We are witnesses', say the Christians. One way in which Paul describes this resurrection is that it was 'the first fruits of those who have fallen asleep'. Here is the beginning of the End. God *will* defeat this evil in His creation and Christ's resurrection is the first tangible evidence of it. God is all-powerful: just because He has not yet fully revealed that power, are we to say 'He doesn't put wrong things right'?

[1] See, for instance, Michael Green, *Man Alive* (Inter-Varsity Press, 1967).

For the Christian there is even more to this. For Paul says 'If the Spirit of him who raised Jesus from the dead dwells in you, he . . . will give life to your mortal bodies also through his Spirit'.[2] The gift of the Holy Spirit is particularly connected with the resurrection. The Spirit which God gives to believers is the resurrection-Spirit. Small wonder, then, if the Christian is able to face the evil in the world with a steady eye and a calm heart. For the Spirit within him is that Spirit of power which raised Jesus from the dead and turned his suffering into glory. This is not an argument, it is an experience. Just as for the disciples in Galilee, the kingdom of God has drawn very close: the last things are here.

This explains why a Christian is able to go on believing in a loving God while living in an evil world. At the beginning of his Christian life it is by faith; he must *believe* that God is loving. But as his life goes on and as he observes other Christians, he comes to *know* that God is loving by experiencing the resurrection-Spirit within him. The man who has passed through the valley of the shadow of death does not debate the problem of evil. He asserts with peaceful simplicity, 'Thou art with me: thy rod and thy staff comfort me'.

God does exist. God does love me. God is with me.

QUESTIONS FOR FURTHER THOUGHT AND DISCUSSION

Why do we have such an inordinate fear of death if nothing lies beyond?

When men's lives make 'most sense' when expressed in a teleological way, isn't it very odd to assert that the whole universe is meaningless in terms of final purpose?

[2] Romans 8:11.